ESSENTIAL
FENG SHUI

SIMON BROWN

WARD LOCK

To my father Michael John Hilton Brown

A WARD LOCK BOOK
This edition first published in the United Kingdom by
Ward Lock
Wellington House
125 Strand
London WC2R 0BB

A Cassell imprint

First published 1999
Reprinted 2000,2002

Created and produced by
CARROLL & BROWN LIMITED
20 Lonsdale Road
London NW6 6RD

The material in this edition was first published in *Practical Feng Shui* 1997

British Library Catalogue-in-Publication Data
A catalogue record for this book is available from
the British Library

ISBN 0-7063-7854-7

Reproduced by Colourscan
Printed and bound in Great Britain by Bath Press Group

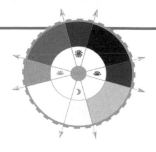

CONTENTS

FENG SHUI TODAY

Feng Shui originated in China over 4000 years ago and its practice has a long history throughout the East. Similar ideas have also existed in other parts of the world at one time or another. The notion that the 'spirit' or atmosphere of a place has an effect on your well-being is widely accepted, but in Feng Shui it has developed into a complex and integrated system of theory and practice embracing almost every aspect of people's lives.

The Chinese characters for 'Feng Shui' translate as 'wind and water'. Feng Shui is actually the art of designing your home to promote success in life, health, wealth and happiness.

The underlying premise of Feng Shui is that everything in your overall and immediate surroundings – even down to the smallest details of furnishing and decor – can either further your aims in life or work against you. By understanding the subtle currents of energy (known throughout this book as 'chi') that flow through your body and through everything in the universe, you can arrange your living and working environments to help you reach your goals.

POTENTIAL BENEFITS OF FENG SHUI

- Improved health
- More harmonious family relationships
- Better relaxation at home
- Better sleep
- More stimulating social life

- Greater opportunities for love and romance
- More active sex life
- Improved chances of becoming pregnant
- Feeling more in control
- Increased motivation

- Increased fame and respect
- Greater control over money matters
- Increased likelihood of selling a home

the PRINCIPLES of FENG SHUI

The concepts of chi energy, yin
and yang, the Five Elements and
the Eight Directions explain
how making changes to your
living space can transform your
life and fortunes.

chi energy

'Chi' is a subtle flow of electromagnetic energy which links all things in the universe. In the Far East the understanding and control of energy flows underlies traditional healing systems such as acupuncture and Shiatsu as well as martial arts like Tai Chi, Qi Kong and Aikido. The energy has several names. In China it is called Chi, in Japan it is known as Ki (also spelt Qi) and in India Prana. There are no specific words for it in the West, although expressions such as 'atmosphere', 'mood', 'life-force' or 'spirit' describe how it is perceived. In this book it is referred to as chi energy. Chi is central to Eastern astrology and Feng Shui.

Chi stays mainly within entities such as human bodies, plants or buildings, but some of it constantly flows out and some flows in from other sources. Your own personal chi energy is always mixing with the chi energy around you. In this way you are connected to the immediate environment, and ultimately to the whole universe, as ripples of chi energy from far away reach you and you send ripples back again. Exceptionally sensitive people may be able to pick up advance information from these distant sources in the form of premonitions, visions or telepathy.

WIND AND WATER

The flow of chi energy from one entity to another is the basis of Feng Shui. The chi energy you take in from your environment influences your moods, emotions, physical energy and, over time, your health. Chi energy is carried through the environment by wind, water, the sun's energy, light and sound. It moves in a similar way to these natural phenomena except that, unlike some of them, it is able to flow through solid matter. It flows in and out of buildings mainly through the doors and windows, but some chi can enter and leave through the walls. It moves like water ebbing and flowing with the tides, and like wind moving around the Earth. The basic aim of Feng Shui is to enable you to position yourself where this natural flow of chi energy helps you to realise your goals and your dreams in life.

Heaven and Earth's forces
Chi energy radiating from the planets moves towards the Earth – Heaven's force. Earth radiates chi energy that moves away from it – Earth's force.

UNIVERSAL CHI

Chi energy flows not only throughout our planet, but through the entire solar system and galaxy. Our own planet, Earth, radiates chi energy that flows out and away from the planet. This appears to us as chi energy moving upwards and is called Earth's force. At the same time, the planets surrounding Earth radiate chi energy which travels towards and into the Earth. This appears to us to move downwards and is known as Heaven's force. So the movement of chi energy on the surface of the Earth, and therefore in our homes and in our own bodies, is influenced by the Earth itself and the surrounding planets. As the position of the Earth, Sun and planets changes, so does the movement of chi energy, which in turn affects our own flow of chi energy.

As Heaven's chi reaches Earth its movement is altered by the landscape (hills, mountains, rivers), vegetation (trees, crops, grasses, bushes) and the ground itself (rocks, clay, soil, chalk). As Earth's force and Heaven's force mix across the surface of the planet, various unique flows of chi energy begin to develop. The same is true of buildings in a city. Low flat dwellings, skyscrapers, pointed roofs, domes and tree-lined avenues all determine how chi energy flows across the surface, and roads, railways, offices, factories, homes, entertainment centres, churches, graveyards and hospitals all have an influence on the nature of that energy.

CHI IN BUILDINGS

Buildings alter the flow of chi energy. Their shape, openings and the materials they are made of define the way chi energy flows through them. It moves most easily through doors and to a lesser extent through windows, so the orientation of a building to the sun and the planets will determine the kind of chi energy that enters it. This changes as the planets move through the sky, so there is a new pattern of chi energy each year, month, day and hour. Features of the immediate surroundings, such as water or roads, further determine the kind of chi energy that flows back and forth through the doors of the building. In an ideal situation chi energy flows harmoniously through the whole of a building. The design and interior decoration should enhance the kind of chi energy that furthers the aims and desires of the occupants and should exclude or minimize features that hinder them.

UNFAVOURABLE CHI ENERGIES

Some situations produce unhelpful types of chi, causing problems for a building's occupants, and even physical or mental ill-health.

NEGATIVE CHI   Certain building or decorating materials have a negative effect on chi energy: synthetic fibres, synthetic building materials, artificial lighting and air conditioning all add their own artificial chi energy, which negatively influences the chi energy of the occupants, and could lead to mental and physical exhaustion.

STAGNANT CHI   Slow-moving and stagnant chi energy is produced by dark corners, cluttered rooms and dampness. They can lead to a slowing down of your own chi energy, which may cause serious health problems and a loss of direction in your life.

FAST-FLOWING CHI   Chi energy moving quickly in a straight line can destabilize the flow through an entire building, so long corridors, straight paths or several features in a straight line should be avoided. Fast-moving chi energy directed towards you could push away some of your own chi energy, making you feel insecure and under attack. (See also Cutting Chi below.)

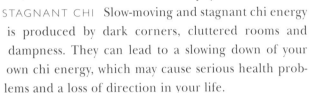

Furniture
Sharp corners on furniture can cause cutting chi. Avoid them in bedrooms and near seating areas.

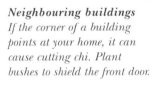

Neighbouring buildings
If the corner of a building points at your home, it can cause cutting chi. Plant bushes to shield the front door.

CUTTING CHI

If chi energy passes a sharp corner it begins to spin and swirl, forming eddies and whirlpools like a fast-flowing stream passing a sharp bend. This is called cutting chi and can occur inside or outside buildings. It can make your own chi energy swirl, leading to disorientation and confusion and, in time, ill-health. Plants and fabrics can be used to 'soften' sharp edges.

PERSONAL CHI

Along the centre of the body are seven concentrations of energy called chakras (see right), which are similar to large organs where blood concentrates. Spreading out from the chakras are 14 paths of chi energy known as meridians. These flow along your arms, legs, torso and head. Like blood vessels and capillaries, they take chi energy to smaller and smaller channels until each cell is nourished by both blood and chi energy.

While blood carries oxygen and nutrients, chi energy carries thoughts, emotions and your dreams in life. It also carries some of the chi energy from the environment. Therefore, what you think and where you think it, will have a direct influence on the cells in your body.

Chi energy operates as a two-way process whereby the way you think influences your chi energy, and your chi energy influences the way you think; so your environment will influence your chi energy and that change will alter the way you think and feel.

Like trees planted in the best soil for their needs, we also thrive if we are planted in an environment that has the most appropriate chi energy. By moving from one building to another, one city to another, or one country to another, you have the opportunity to change your own chi energy and therefore the way you think and feel. If the chi energy of the place where you live matches the chi energy you require for happiness, then it will have a very positive influence on your life. Unfortunately, it is also possible that your home may work against you, and the chi energy of some places could negatively affect your well-being.

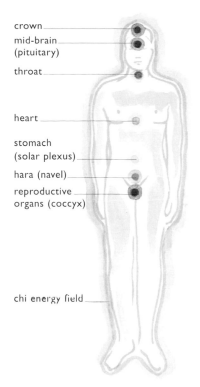

crown
mid-brain (pituitary)
throat
heart
stomach (solar plexus)
hara (navel)
reproductive organs (coccyx)
chi energy field

The chakras
Chi flows through the human body by means of channels called meridians which act rather like blood vessels. They radiate from seven key points in the body where energy concentrates, called chakras. Typically, chi extends at least 10cm and up to 1 metre outside your skin.

Many factors affect the chi energy that comes into your body – among these are food, weather and the people you are with. In Feng Shui terms, the primary influence is the chi energy of the environment. This includes your home, your place of work and the surrounding landscape. A building itself has an influence. Being in a large ornate building such as a museum or cathedral can be inspiring, exciting and stimulating, whereas a small cosy place such as a cottage or bar is more relaxing and intimate. A building's location also helps shape the kind of chi that enters your body, as different landscapes have different kinds of chi.

yin and yang

The concept of yin and yang offers a comprehensive way of looking at the world and how it affects you. It makes it possible to adjust your relationship with people and your surroundings so that you can place yourself in favourable rather than unfavourable situations. Ultimately, you will be able to use your knowledge of yin and yang to get more out of your life with less effort.

At the time of a full moon, for example, people become more yang, which means they are more active, want to go out more and are generally more sociable. Conversely, at the time of a new moon they become more yin – more peaceful, spiritual, relaxed and inward-looking. So if you want to organize a party, the days before or during the full moon are the best times. People will be more outgoing and more in the mood for a get-together. At the new moon you risk fewer people turning up and those who do will be quieter.

basic principles

EVERYTHING IS EITHER MORE YIN OR MORE YANG

Yin and yang are relative terms used to compare everything in the universe. Things are more yin or more yang depending on what they are compared with. For example, resting is more yin than working, but more yang than sleeping. Yin and yang can describe physical things or non-physical things. You need to be clear about how the terms are applied in particular cases. For example, a flame is more yang than a stone in terms of a process: the flame produces heat and light. But the structure of stone is more yang than flame: more solid and harder.

EVERYTHING SEEKS A STATE OF BALANCE

Although everything is either more yin or more yang, as an entity it seeks some kind of balance. Individually nothing is in perfect balance, nor can it be as everything is either more yin or more yang. Something that is more yin can reach a more balanced state with something that is more yang. Often we drift either side of the middle path. For a while we become more yin and then make changes that make us more yang, and vice versa.

Similar principles can be applied to your home, diet, exercise, work and leisure activities. They all have aspects that are more yin or more yang, and you can encourage them to work for you or against you depending on your needs at the time.

GLOBAL YIN AND YANG

The position of the sun and moon, and the seasons make you feel more yin or yang, and you instinctively adjust your lifestyle to keep a balance.

Yin and yang in time
The environment is most yang at midday, in high summer and at full moon. It is most yin at midnight, in midwinter and at the new moon.

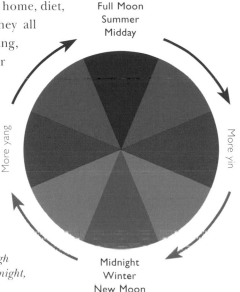

Full Moon
Summer
Midday

More yang

More yin

Midnight
Winter
New Moon

YIN AND YANG ATTRACT EACH OTHER

Things that are more yin attract other things that are more yang, rather like the poles of a magnet. As you become more yin you attract things that are more yang into your life and vice versa. A simple example is that by eating something more yang, such as dry salty snacks, you begin to crave liquids, which are more yin. An extreme of yin or yang will attracts its extreme opposite. For example, someone who becomes very yang – angry or aggressive – may end up in a very yin state – confined in hospital or prison (because of an accident or crime).

NOTHING IS WHOLLY YIN OR WHOLLY YANG

Everything has some yin and some yang. Nothing is entirely one thing or the other, though everything will be more one thing or another. It is better to think of yin and yang in terms of varying shades of grey, rather than black and white. Even the most ruthless criminal will have a tender spot just as the gentlest person will have known frustration and anger. There is always something positive in a negative situation just as there is something negative in a positive situation.

EVERYTHING CHANGES

The relationships between things that are more yin and things that are more yang are constantly changing. Everything is always moving from being more yang to being more yin or more yin to more yang. For example a person might be more yang – irritable, frustrated and pushy – but in the process of becoming more yin – relaxed, peaceful and calm. In the long term the direction you are going is more important than where you are now.

YIN AND YANG IN THE HOME

The sun's movement through the sky alters the flow of chi energy through your home. As the sun rises through the sky from morning to midday, the east, south-east and south of your home will become energized by more yang chi energy. In the southern hemisphere this will be the east, north-east and north of your home. After midday as the sun descends in the sky, the west, north-west and north of your home are energized by more yin chi energy. In the southern hemisphere this will be the west, south-west and south.

To check these directions, take a compass and stand in the centre of your home. Move around until you have a consistent compass reading. The needle of your compass will be pointing north. Alternatively, watch the sun move through the sky. Wait until it reaches the highest point. If you are in the northern hemisphere the sun is now south of your home; in the southern hemisphere it will be to the north.

The sunny side of your home is better for activities that require you to be more yang. The shady side is better for those that require you to be more yin. If you are already too yin or too yang, spend more time in a place that has the opposite type of chi energy in order to become more balanced. For example, if you get angry quickly and have difficulty relaxing you could be too yang and should spend more time in the yin side of your home. If you move your bedroom to a yin part of the building you will be taking in more peaceful yin chi energy as you sleep and this will counter your more yang tendencies when you get angry.

On the other hand, if you feel tired, depressed and tearful you could be too yin. Work or do things in the sunny side of your home to take in more yang chi energy. The effect of yin and yang on the different parts of your home will also influence how you allocate the various rooms there.

Yin and yang shapes
Tall thin and long narrow buildings are more yin, low squat buildings in compact shapes such as squares, circles and octagons are more yang.

PERSONAL YIN AND YANG

People can be more yin or more yang. More yin people tend to be relaxed, physically supple, sensitive, creative and imaginative. However, if they are too yin, they can be lethargic, slow and prone to depression. Conversely, more yang people tend to be alert, quick, more active, and more able to concentrate and pay attention to detail. If they are too yang they can become tense and irritable, angry or physically stiff and tight.

ARE YOU TOO YIN OR TOO YANG?

One way to assess this is to compare yourself to other people. When you are too yin, other people will seem more aggressive, irritable and impatient with you. They will want you to hurry, while you want to relax and take things easy. When you are too yang, you will find other people slow, indecisive and quiet. You may find yourself becoming irritable and angry with them. Some people are always more yin than most people, some are always more yang, and others will be more in the middle.

With an understanding of yin and yang you can adjust these natural tendencies to your advantage by tailoring your diet (macrobiotics is specially designed for this) and lifestyle. If you find it difficult to concentrate, for example, and your work is suffering, decide first if you are too yin or too yang. Concentration is a more yang activity, so a lack of it suggests you are too yin. The solution would be to avoid more yin foods such as alcohol, sugar and coffee, and include some mineral-rich yang foods, such as root vegetables, fish and natural soya sauce.

Yin and yang food
Eating the right kinds of food can help balance your personal levels of yin and yang. The foods above range from the most yang (salt and meat) at the top to the most yin (liquids and sugars) at the bottom.

yin and yang in your home

The shapes, materials and colours of objects you put in your home make the chi energy there more yin or more yang. This provides you with ways to alter the chi energy of your home to suit your needs.

SHAPES

Rounded shapes are generally considered to be more yin than straight-sided shapes – a long thin curved table is more yin than a rectangular table. A circle is the exception because, although it is rounded, it is also the most compact shape and is therefore more yang. Objects that are compact with straight or angular lines are also more yang in shape.

COLOURS

Colours have a great influence on yin and yang by reflecting different frequencies of light back into the room. People react to colours in a very personal way, but in general red, orange and bright yellow make us feel more yang, greens and blues more yin. Pastel shades of any colour are more yin than stronger brighter shades of that colour. The larger the area covered by a particular colour the greater its influence will be. Even small touches of strong bright colours, such as scarlet or purple, however, can be effective.

MORE YANG
SHAPES
Circular
Octagonal
Square
Broad rectangle
Broad oval
Long thin rectangle
Thin and wavy
MORE YIN
SHAPES

MORE YANG
COLOURS
Red
Orange
Yellow
Green
Blue
MORE YIN
COLOURS

MORE YANG
FLOORS
Marble
Stone
Hardwoods
Softwoods
Cork tiles
Rush matting
Rugs
Carpets
MORE YIN
FLOORS

Yin and yang objects
*Colour can make things more yin
(blues, greens) or more yang (reds,
oranges, yellows).*

A painting which includes a patch of
brilliant red can change the chi
energy of an entire room.

MATERIALS

What things are made of – especially
the type of material and finish of their
surfaces – encourages either a quicker
more yang flow of chi energy or a slower
more yin flow. Generally, hard and shiny,
reflective surfaces such as glass, polished
marble or stainless steel speed up the flow of
chi energy, whereas soft, matt or textured surfaces such as natural wood and fabric slow it down.

MORE YANG WINDOW TREATMENTS	MORE YANG FURNISHINGS	MORE YANG MATERIALS
Shutters	Stone sculptures	Glass
Metal slatted blinds	Mirrors	Marble
Wooden slatted blinds	Varnished paintings	Granite
Paper blinds	Metal furniture	Polished stone
Cloth blinds	Hardwood furniture	Unpolished stone
Short curtains	Softwood furniture	Shiny metal
Unlined long curtains	Paper screens	Dull metal
Full draped curtains	Upholstered furniture	Polished hardwoods
	Tapestries	Natural hardwoods
	Large cushions	Polished softwoods
		Natural softwoods
		Wicker
		Fabric
MORE YIN WINDOW TREATMENTS	MORE YIN FURNISHINGS	MORE YIN MATERIALS

five elements

The Five Elements are associated with five directions that are related to the movement of the sun. In the morning the east of your home soaks up the upward chi, known as tree energy. As the day progresses, the sun moves from east to south so that the south of your home radiates with fire energy. Later, the sun starts to set and brings more settled soil chi energy into the south-west and centre of your home. As the sun sets, the west of your home takes in inward-moving metal chi energy. During the night, the north of your home benefits from flowing water chi energy.

These five energies are taken into your home most intensively at the relevant times of day and remain there until recharged again the following day. So the east of your home, for example, will always be charged to some extent with tree energy regardless of the time of day.

The Five Elements are also found in your home in their pure form. Tree energy is there in the form of wood, paper and tall plants; fire in the form of stoves, fireplaces and lighting; soil in the form of china, clay

five-element chi energies

The concept of the Five Elements is a refinement of the principle of yin and yang. Instead of two types of chi energy, there are five: tree, fire, soil, metal and water.

Tree *Imagine walking down a tree-lined path in the early morning in spring as the sun starts to rise. The overriding feeling is of energy moving up, like the branches of a tree reaching up into the sky. The tree is coming into leaf.*

Fire *It is the middle of a hot summer's day. Nature is in full bloom. The tree is in full leaf. Bright light and colourful flowers fill the picture. The energy seems to expand in every direction, radiating like the heat of a glowing fire.*

and plaster; metal in the form of iron, silver, stainless steel and other metals; water in the form of fountains, sinks, bathrooms and aquariums.

SHAPES, COLOURS AND MATERIALS

The Five Elements are associated with shapes, colours and materials (see chart on page 18) and, in this way, can be introduced into your home and applied to the building itself. Wallpaper with vertical stripes, for example, will bring more uplifting tree chi energy, making the ceiling appear higher and the room taller. Strong colours like red and black will be effective even when they cover a relatively small surface area, such as a vase of red flowers. Similarly, the material your furniture is made of – wood or metal, for example – will adjust the atmosphere.

These effects will be especially intense if you combine colours with particular patterns or materials. For example, green wallpaper with vertical stripes would represent tree energy and so on. This ability to manipulate the existing chi energy using the Five Elements is the basis of many Feng Shui remedies.

Soil *Think of an afternoon in early autumn. The leaves have changed colour and are beginning to fall. The sun is getting lower in the sky. The overall feeling is of energy moving down into the ground.*

Metal *It is evening in late autumn. As the red sun sinks below the horizon the feeling is of energy gathering in, and nature storing up its energy ready for the winter. Energy is moving inwards and becoming solid.*

Water *Imagine a damp, frosty night in midwinter. All is still on the surface, but powerful changes are taking place below the soil and there are strong currents of water beneath the ice. Water is calm on the surface but flowing beneath.*

FIVE ELEMENT	SHAPES/COLOURS		MATERIALS	MEANING
TREE East/South-east	rectangular tall thin vertical	green	wood wicker rush bamboo paper	life growth vitality activity
FIRE South	pointed star serrated triangular pyramid diamond zigzag	red	(plastic is the material associated with fire chi energy, but is not recommended for use in the home because of its negative effects on chi energy – see also page 78)	passion warmth excitement expression
SOIL South-west/Centre/ North-east	squat low flat wide check horizontal	yellow brown	plaster china clay ceramic brick natural fibres softer stone (e.g. limestone)	comfort security steadiness caution
METAL West/North-west	round domed arched oval circular spherical	white gold silver	stainless steel brass silver bronze copper iron gold	richness solidity leadership organization
WATER North	irregular curved chaotic wavy amorphous	black	glass	depth power flexibility tranquillity

FIVE-ELEMENT RELATIONSHIPS

Two flows of chi energy govern the relationships between the Five Elements: the support cycle and the destructive or control cycle. These can be compared to the annual agricultural cycle as each of the Five Elements relates to a particular season: water to winter, tree to spring, fire to summer, soil to early autumn, metal to late autumn.

WATER Winter is when the ground is prepared and seeds are planted. If spring is fine, the seeds grow. But if there are late frosts, new shoots are destroyed. Water supports tree, but if tree is deficient, water destroys fire. Think of water feeding a tree, but extinguishing fire.

TREE If spring goes well, the fields are full of crops in summer. But if summer is poor due to lack of sun or heavy rains, the crops rot in the ground in the early autumn. Tree supports fire, as wood is fuel but, if fire is deficient, tree destroys soil.

FIRE After a good summer the crops ripen in early autumn. If the weather is cold and cloudy in early autumn, the crops will not ripen in time for the late autumn harvest. Fire supports soil just as ash enriches the earth but, if soil is deficient, fire can destroy metal.

SOIL Plenty of sun in early autumn means a good harvest. But early frosts or heavy rain in late autumn destroys the harvest and there are no new seeds to plant in the winter. Soil supports metal just as minerals in the soil form metal ores, but if metal is deficient, soil will destroy water.

METAL If the crop has set seed in the late autumn and conditions in winter are good, the seed can be planted for the following spring. But harsh winter conditions may destroy the seed before it can to sprout. Metal supports water, but if water is deficient metal will destroy tree.

5 ELEMENT	SUPPORTS	DESTROYS	DRAINS
WATER	tree	fire (if tree is weak)	metal
TREE	fire	soil (if fire is weak)	water
FIRE	soil	metal (if soil is weak)	tree
SOIL	metal	water (if metal is weak)	fire
METAL	water	tree (if water is weak)	soil

USING THE FIVE ELEMENTS

The Five Elements and the relationships between them provide a model for understanding the universe and the interaction of the different types of chi energy. They can be used to manipulate the flow of chi in your home and are the basis of many Feng Shui remedies and solutions. Depending on what you are trying to achieve or what problem you are trying to solve, you can enhance one type of Five Element chi energy, calm another or maintain a balance by introducing objects associated with the relevant elements (see below) into the appropriate space.

Five-Element chi energies can be introduced into a space in pure form – actual plants, fire, soil, metal or water – or in the form of representative objects. The most powerful objects are those which combine the shape, colour and material of an element (for example, round, silver, metal balls for metal energy, or a low, brown, terracotta trough filled with brown earth for soil energy).

introducing five-element objects

Water
Use clean fresh water itself, glass objects or things that are black or irregular in shape. Those above include glass dishes and pebbles, black wavy stems and fabric.

Tree
Use actual plants, wood or paper and tall, thin green objects. Those above include a green pot, a tall green vase, tall lamp with paper shade and green frame.

Suppose you have a room in the south of your home, and you wish to increase the chi energy there to feel more expressive. The south is linked with fire chi energy. Fire is supported by tree energy. So you can boost the chi energy of the south by building up fire energy itself or by adding supportive tree energy. Fire energy is linked with pointed shapes, the colour red, lights and fire itself, so to boost it introduce candles, red star-patterned wallpaper and bright lights into the room.

Tree chi energy is linked with tall thin rectangular shapes, the colour green and materials wood and paper. Trees and tall plants are the element itself, so tall plants, green vertical-striped wallpaper, wooden floors and a paper screen all increase tree chi energy in the room.

To reduce the chi energy in a southern room you would need to bolster the Five-Element chi energy that is draining to fire, namely soil. Low clay sculptures, the colour yellow, and low spreading plants growing in plenty of soil would bring more soil chi energy into the room.

Fire
Use fire itself and red or pointed objects. Those above include an oil lamp, star-shaped candle holders, a red star, red flowers in a red vase and red fabric.

Soil
Use soil or clay itself and yellow or brown or low rectangular objects. Those above include a clay trough, yellow flowers, a square plate, frame and checked fabric.

Metal
Use metal itself and round, silver, gold or white objects. Those above include a round metal frame, a round metal pot, a round wire tray and silvery balls.

eight directions

The principle of the Eight Directions takes yin and yang and the Five Elements a step further by identifying eight different kinds of chi energy. These eight different kinds of chi energy are each associated with the eight directions of the compass. Each direction is also linked with a trigram from the *I Ching* (see below), a Five Element, a symbol of the natural world, a colour, a time of day and a season. Together these all produce a detailed picture of the type of chi energy found in that particular direction.

TRIGRAMS The author of an ancient Chinese philosophical text called the *I Ching* devised the trigrams. Each trigram consists of three broken or solid lines (representing yin and yang respectively), symbolizing a particular combination of energies. For example, the trigram for water is a solid line at the centre with a broken line above and below. The lines represent an energy that is outwardly flexible and quiet (yin) but with deep strength inside (yang).

FIVE ELEMENTS Each direction and the centre is linked to at least one of the Five Elements (see pages 16–21). The north and south each have their own Five Element, the other directions all share a Five Element.

SYMBOLS Where two directions share a Five Element, they each have a different symbol. For example, the east and south-east share Five Element tree, so they each have a different symbol: thunder in the east and wind in the south-east.

COLOUR Each direction and the centre has a colour associated with it. The colours of the east, south-east and centre are the same as those linked with the Five Elements; the rest are different.

TIME OF DAY This is determined by the time when the sun is in the relevant direction. The chi energy there is strongest at that time, so the chi energy in the south of your home is strongest at midday.

SEASON Each direction is linked with a season and this is when the chi energy there will be strongest. For example, chi energy in the south of your home is strongest in midsummer.

CHI OF THE CENTRE This ninth type of chi energy holds the greatest power, implying greater possibilities, but also greater risks. It is changeable with two extremes: productive and destructive. It is linked with the Five Element soil, the number five and the colour yellow.

the eight types of chi energy

A distinctive type of energy is found in different sectors of a home, room or landscape. These sectors are defined by their direction from the centre of the home, room or landscape, which is determined by an ordinary compass (see pages 26–30). A room in the north of your home, for example, carries the chi energy of the north, but different parts of that room also hold elements of chi energies of the other directions. Eight Directions chi energies include yin and yang, the Five Elements, and the other associations defined opposite. The diagram below summarizes the general picture and the chart overleaf describes the implications for each type of chi energy in detail.

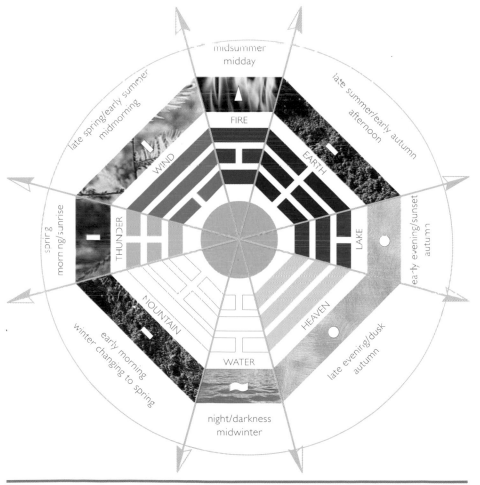

DIRECTION	CHI ENERGY

NORTH

 Trigram yin/yang/yin
Five Element water
Symbol water
Colour off-white
Time of day night/darkness
Season midwinter

North represents conception – life beginning – when the child begins to develop its individual characteristics in its mother's womb, almost independent of the outside world. On the surface all seems quiet, but inside powerful changes are taking place. The chi energy is quiet and most active at night and in midwinter. It relates to sex, spirituality and isolation. Water chi energy also implies depth and movement with flexibility. It can change direction easily, but this is done in a less disruptive way than with other types of chi energy. Off-white has an almost translucent quality most easily produced with a gloss finish.

NORTH-EAST

 Trigram yang/yin/yin
Five Element soil
Symbol mountain
Colour brilliant white
Time of day early morning
Season winter changing to spring

This is when the child learns to interact with the world. It develops individuality, competitiveness directed at survival and preparing for the next phase, along with strength and stubbornness. The north-east is part of a north-east/south-west axis where both directions and the centre have the same Five Element – soil. Energy can move very quickly because it does not have to transform into another element – making these directions unstable. North-east chi is strong, piercing and quick to change direction. It is most active just before dawn and towards the end of winter. The mountain symbolizes a rocky harshness.

EAST

 Trigram yin/yin/yang
Five Element tree
Symbol thunder
Colour green
Time morning/sunrise
Season spring

In this phase the child is ready to embark on a career. It is a time of ambition and new beginnings. The chi energy is active and focussed – and most intense at sunrise. The trigram has a solid yang line beneath two broken yin lines, allowing the yang energy to move forcefully up through the yin lines before retreating to a more tranquil state. The tree provides an upward thrusting energy, and the image of sunrise adds the idea that it is the beginning of a new day. Thunder provides great power, aggression and the urge to go out and make things happen. This energy is also linked with ambition and realising dreams.

SOUTH-EAST

Trigram yang/yang/yin
Five Element tree
Symbol wind
Colour dark green/blue
Time of day mid-morning
Season late spring/early summer

This phase of maturity and harmonious progress is when long-term relationships are formed, including engagements and marriage. The chi energy here is busy and active, but less sharp than that of the east. It is strongest in mid-morning and early summer when the sun is rising in the sky. The trigram has a yin line sitting beneath two yang lines. Gentleness at the heart is protected by great activity on the surface. The symbol of wind brings persistence and power to this chi energy, but is less aggressive and dramatic than thunder. Dark green symbolizes growth and vitality, but a more established kind than the east.

DIRECTION	CHI ENERGY

SOUTH

Trigram yang/yin/ yang
Five Element fire
Symbol fire
Colour purple
Time of day midday
Season midsummer

This phase represents the prime of life when hard work has paid off and the benefits of success can at last be enjoyed. The chi energy of the south is fiery, passionate and brilliant, and is most active at midday and in midsummer when the sun is at its highest point. If the chi energy in this part of a home is moving well, fame and social success could be the result. The trigram is a yin line sandwiched between two yang lines. The chi energy is active and dynamic on the surface, but flexible and flowing on the inside. It is also linked with intelligence and beauty. The colour purple instils passion, excitement and heat.

SOUTH-WEST

Trigram yin/yin/yin
Five Element soil
Symbol earth
Colour black
Time of day afternoon
Season late summer/early autumn

This chi energy is symbolized by the more settled state of middle age – a state usually associated with spending more time at home – and family harmony is the dominant theme. This chi energy is most active in the afternoon and late summer as the sun sinks in the sky, providing an atmosphere that is conducive to consolidation and methodical progress. The trigram has three yin lines, implying a more receptive, yielding, motherly energy. The symbol of the earth carries the idea of supporting and nourishing life. Black, like the colour of rich, dark soil, enhances the atmosphere of nurturing and supportiveness.

WEST

Trigram yin/yang/ yang
Five element metal
Symbol lake
Colour red
Time of day sunset
Season autumn

This is the time of late middle age approaching retirement and is associated with relaxing and enjoying the fruits of your labours. Most active at sunset and in autumn, the chi energy of the west is linked with financial income and the harvest. The trigram has a yin line over two yang lines. The calm of the surface is supported by strength below, which creates a playful movement of chi energy. The lake brings a deeper, more reflective quality, and metal energy is associated with material wealth and style. Red is like the fiery glow of a brilliant sunset and enhances feelings of romance and contentment.

NORTH-WEST
Trigram yang/yang/ yang
Five Element metal
Symbol heaven
Colour silver white
Time of day dusk
Season late autumn/winter

This is the final phase in the cycle of life. By this time the accumulation of experience has led to wisdom, and the possibility of helping others and being a mentor through the earlier stages. The chi energy of the north-west is linked with leadership, organization and planning ahead, and is most active at dusk and in late autumn or winter. The three yang lines of the trigram bring a powerful, fatherly chi energy. The symbol of heaven adds dignity, wisdom and an image of superiority. The association of the colour silvery white with the hair of an elderly person reinforces the impression of dignity, respect and wisdom.

tools of feng shui

To apply the principles of Feng Shui to your home you first need to assess the pattern of chi energies there. This involves finding out which parts of your home fall in which directions, and therefore which parts are characterized by the different types of chi energy. In order to do this you must have a detailed and accurate floor plan of your home on which to align a grid of the Eight Directions. If one is already available, make sure all details relevant to Feng Shui considerations are marked on it (see right). If not you will need to draw one up yourself.

"Your home" in this context refers to the space you own, rent or occupy. It could be a house or apartment. If it is an apartment, the plan should cover only those areas of the building that are yours, for your sole use. Later, you can assess the apartment within the whole building.

equipment

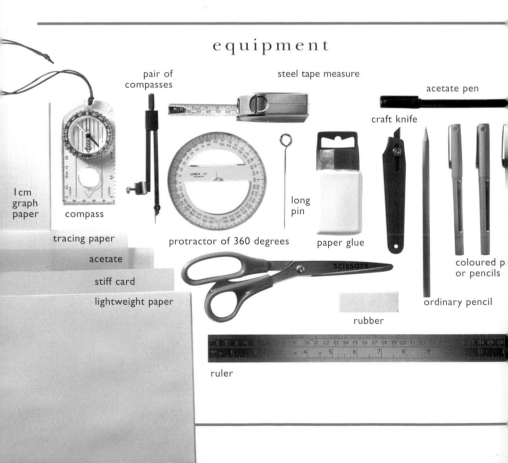

pair of
compasses

steel tape measure

acetate pen

craft knife

1 cm
graph
paper

compass

long
pin

tracing paper

protractor of 360 degrees

paper glue

acetate

coloured p
or pencils

stiff card

scissors

lightweight paper

ordinary pencil

rubber

ruler

THE FENG SHUI FLOOR PLAN

If your home has more than one floor, make a separate plan for each one. Draw them to scale using graph paper to make the job easier (see below). Include all the internal walls, all doors, windows, staircases, fireplaces, and mark likely problem features such as protruding corners, sloping roofs or overhead beams. Fixed features that are important in Feng Shui terms, namely, fireplaces, sinks, fixed cookers, baths, showers and lavatories, should also be marked. Finally, indicate the likely positions of movable items such as beds, chairs, sofas and dining tables.

The next step is to find the centre of your home (see page 28) and of all the main rooms (especially where they are used for more than one function such as kitchen/dining rooms). Finally, align the plan with the grid of the Eight Directions (see page 29). This will enable you to assess the balance of chi energies in your home at a glance.

drawing a floor plan

MEASURING THE ROOMS

Using a long retractable steel measure, note the length and width of each floor of your home, then of each room, and of staircases and corridors. Measure into alcoves and bay windows if appropriate.

Convert the measurements to a convenient scale, eg, 1 metre = 1 cm. So if your room measures 5.2 x 3.5 metres, the rectangle on the plan would have to measure 5.2 x 3.5 cm.

Transfer the measurements to the plan in the appropriate positions. In scale, add to the plan all windows, doors, fitted store cupboards, wardrobes and kitchen units. Indicate on the plan the way the doors open.

Adding relevant features
Mark on the plan all details relevant in Feng Shui terms (see above). Mark the fixed features in one colour, the movable ones in another, and the problem features in a third colour.

finding the centre

To determine the directions on your floor plan, first find the centre of each floor and of each of the main rooms. The easiest shapes to handle are simple squares and rectangles. Irregular shapes are rather more complicated. There is a mathematical method for finding the centre of irregular shapes, but the easiest way is to find the balancing point of the shape using a long pin.

Finding the centre of squares and rectangles
Draw lines between opposing corners. The centre of the shape is the point where they intersect.

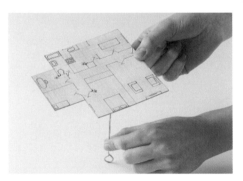

Finding the centre of irregular shapes
Trace the shape of the floor or room, transfer or paste it on to stiff card and cut it out. Hold the card horizontally and try balancing it on the point of a long pin. Move the pin until you find the balancing point. This is the centre of the shape. Transfer it to the floor plan.

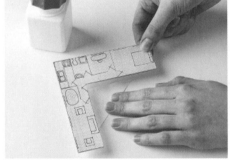

Finding the centre of L-shapes
The balancing point of an L-shape may be outside the shape itself. Glue a piece of lightweight paper over the area between the wings of the building where the centre is likely to be. You can balance the pin on this paper without it affecting the centre of the shape.

aligning the grid of the eight directions

The grid of the Eight Directions is shown on page 30. It includes a marker for magnetic north. Scan the grid into your computer or photocopy it onto transparent film or draw it onto tracing paper using a protractor and ruler. Next align the grid with the floor plan using a compass.

Finding magnetic north on the floor plan
Place the plan on a flat surface so that the walls on the plan align with the same walls in the area you are in. Place the compass on the plan so that its centre is over that of the plan. Turn the compass so the needle lines up with the marker line. Mark the plan at this point and draw a line to the centre.

GETTING A CONSISTENT COMPASS READING

Many objects distort compass readings: things made of iron or steel, electrical appliances, concealed metal beams, water tanks, water or gas pipes. Walk around your home holding the compass steady until the reading is consistent in several parts of a room. If this is not possible indoors try doing it outside. Use the room or space where the reading is consistent to find north on your plan.

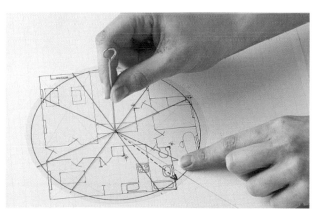

Aligning the grid of the eight directions
Place the transparent grid over the floor plan aligning the centres on both. Push a pin through the centres. Rotate the grid until the line pointing north on the grid aligns with magnetic north on the floor plan underneath. You can now read off the directions in your home through the transparent grid.

the grid of the eight directions

The grid below is used to determine the directions, and therefore the pattern of chi energy in a home (see pages 28–29). Different Feng Shui schools draw up the grid in different ways. I use the system that divides it into four segments of 30 degrees and four of 60 degrees, which synchronizes the Eight Directions with the 12 animals of Chinese astrology.

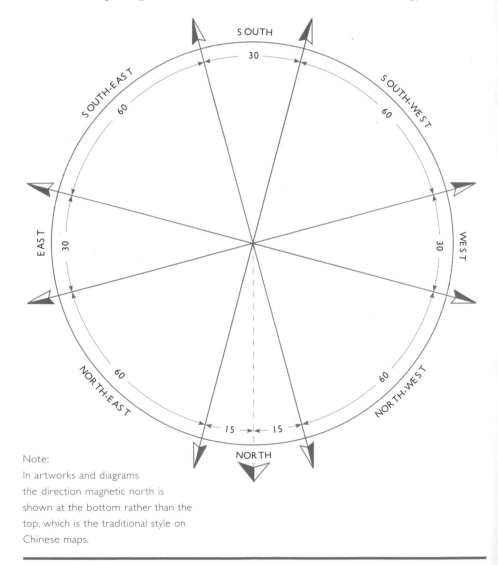

Note:
In artworks and diagrams the direction magnetic north is shown at the bottom rather than the top, which is the traditional style on Chinese maps.

the ROOMS in your HOME

If you place rooms in favourable locations and
choose your furnishings and decor
according to Feng Shui principles,
it can make you happier and more
comfortable in your home,
and generally further your aims in life.

simple feng shui remedies

If the chi energy in a room is not satisfactory for the activities that take place there, it may be impractical to implement any radical solutions such as redecorating or relocating rooms. In such cases there may be some very simple remedies that can be used instead. First, check the room's location. If the direction is not favourable for its function, decide whether the chi energy there needs to be enhanced or calmed. If the chi energy is favourable, simply help to strengthen that beneficial balance.

DIRECTION	ENHANCE CHI	STRENGTHEN CHI	CALM CHI
NORTH	Round silver or iron pot filled with red flowers or a red flowering plant.	Grow ivy or water lilies with white plants. Curved glass statue or crystal.	Tall plants.
NORTH-EAST	Candles. clay container.	White flowers in a low white china bowl.	Sea salt in small round ramekin dish.
EAST	Water feature.	Tall plants.	Candles.
SOUTH-EAST	Water feature.	Tall plants.	Candles.
SOUTH	Tall plants.	Candles. Lights.	Charcoal in a low clay container.
SOUTH-WEST	Candles. Bright lights.	Yellow flowers in a clay container.	Sea salt in a small round ramekin dish.
WEST	Yellow or gold fabrics and colours. Yellow flowers.	Red flowers in a round metal pot. Coins on a red cloth.	Grow ivy or water lilies. Curved glass statue.
NORTH-WEST	Yellow fabrics or flowers.	White flowers in a round silver pot. Clock.	Grow ivy or water lilies. Curved glass statue.
CENTRE	Keep empty.	Keep empty.	Sea salt.

the living room

The living room is central to family life and supports probably the widest range of activities of any room in the home. It is where you entertain your guests, host parties and hold important family celebrations. It is also, often, the place where you relax after a day's work and maybe read a book, watch television or listen to music.

A bright sunny room will help to create a lively uplifting place where you and your family will enjoy spending time together. The sunlight charges up the chi energy and helps to stimulate the flow of energy through the room. South-east is bright and lively. South is favourable for holding parties and large social events. South-west will help create a settled cosy atmosphere. West is good for entertaining and the pursuit of pleasure generally; it also has a romantic character.

Usually the living room is the largest room, and plenty of space is essential to its success. Chi energy can stagnate in overcrowded, claustrophobic rooms. If your potential living room is too small, open out two or more adjoining rooms. It is easier to keep chi energy flowing gently through one large room than through several small ones. Use mirrors where necessary, to adjust the overall proportions of the room and create an illusion of space (see page 90). Long thin rooms and L-shaped rooms can both be improved in this way.

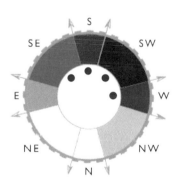

Recommended directions for a living room
South-east, south, south-west and west of the centre of your home.

LIVING/DINING ROOMS

Often, particularly in small apartments, it is practical to combine the living room and dining room. Generally, entertaining and eating are compatible functions, and you can usually create an atmosphere that works for both. Sometimes, the living and dining area also incorporates the kitchen. The main drawback here is that the kitchen part must be kept especially clean and tidy at all times. If not, it has a negative impact on chi energy which can easily spread to the rest of the room. (See pages 40–44 and 55–58 for considerations affecting dining rooms and kitchens.)

an ideal living room

The south-east, a favourable location, is characterized by lively, uplifting Five-Element tree energy. Use decor and furnishings to enhance the living room's spaciousness and to make it feel relaxing and comfortable. At the same time, try to promote sociability and family harmony. To allow chi energy to circulate freely, keep large pieces of furniture to a minimum and do not overuse heavy fabrics and upholstery. Remember to balance the need for comfort against the risk of chi energy stagnating.

THINGS TO AVOID

SPIKY PLANTS Plants with sharp-pointed leaves produce cutting chi, so plants like palms and yuccas should not be placed next to chairs and sofas where people are likely to sit, but ideally in the corners of the room.

CLUTTER To prevent chi energy stagnating, keep living rooms free of household clutter and too many decorative objects. Make sure the centre of the room is relatively empty.

CLOSED CURTAINS To allow energizing sunlight freely into the living room, try to keep curtains wide open during the day, exposing the entire window.

OVER-FURNISHING Chi energy needs space to move so keep furniture to a minimum.

PROTRUDING CORNERS If exposed these can cause cutting chi, so screen them with bushy plants or drape them with fabric.

❶ LIGHTING *The vertical beam of uplighters and the shape of standing lamps supports upward-moving tree energy.*

❷ TELEVISION *Electronic equipment has a negative effect on chi energy. Position the television away from the seating area.*

❸ PLANTS *Use plants to minimize the negative effects of the television. Tall palms strengthen tree chi energy, making the living room more social and exciting. In smaller living rooms, round-leaved bushy plants would be more appropriate.*

❹ SOFAS AND CHAIRS *Arrange seating to promote sociability and family harmony (see pages 38–9). Sofas and chairs placed north-west facing south-east and west facing east are the most favourable positions in this room, resulting in good communication. To promote relaxation, choose living room seating which is more yin – soft and rounded. Rounded shapes also prevent cutting chi. Green and cream are harmonious in the south-east — the more yin pale green helps create a spacious feeling.*

❺ FLOOR COVERING *The stripped wooden floor supports tree energy and generally maintains the harmonious flow of chi energy in the room. The pure wool rug provides comfort while avoiding the risks of stagnation that a fitted carpet would present.*

❻ WINDOW TREATMENT *Fabrics help slow chi energy, which is relaxing and appropriate to a living room. But curtains should not be too full as this risks stagnation.*

❼ WALL COVERING *Vertical stripes support tree energy helping to create an impression of height and space. Patterned walls are more yin, ideal in a living room where relaxation and comfort are important goals.*

❽ PAINTINGS *Cheerful subjects such as a brilliant sunrise have positive psychological effects.*

❾ ACCESSORIES *Choose colours for accessories such as cushions to fine-tune chi energy. Purple calms tree energy.*

CHOOSING THE DECOR

In a south-east living room colours and patterns should aim to maintain the favourable lively chi energy. Dark green is a harmonious colour, but paler, more yin shades are also used to promote relaxation and give the room a light, spacious feel. To calm the chi energy here, use more pale purple; to build it up use more cream and off-white. Shades of blue could be used instead of, or in addition to, green. Vertical patterns such as stripes in green and cream support tree energy. Irregular patterns would be enhancing, pointed ones calming.

DECOR FOR OTHER
FAVOURABLE LOCATIONS

THE SOUTH The fiery chi energy here is warm and sociable, ideal for parties but, perhaps, a little too passionate for everyday relaxation. I recommend that you strengthen the ambient chi energy, but also add calming touches. Softer shades of purple with pale yellow accents will do this.

SOUTH *Pale purple strengthens chi here and yellow calms it.*

THE SOUTH-WEST The main feeling here is settled and domestic which is ideal for a cosy relaxed family living room, but it might need sharpening up for social occasions. You could strengthen the ambient chi energy but add enhancing touches. Earth colours such as yellow and brown are harmonious, and use purple here and there, perhaps, in a pattern on wallpaper or furnishing fabric. Check patterns will strengthen the soil energy here; pointed patterns or shapes, which represent fire chi energy, will enhance it.

SOUTH-WEST *Checked patterns in shades of yellow and brown will strengthen soil energy.*

THE WEST This is a playful, pleasurable location, which favours most of the activities likely to take place in a living room, so an appropriate strategy might simply be to strengthen this natural ambience. Use soft rusty reds and pinks, with occasional touches of grey and white. Rounded patterns – circles, ovals, stylized flowers, waves or scallops – will add to the favourable metal chi energy of the west. Circular cushions in harmonious colours, or round silver or gold plates hung on the walls would have the same effect.

WEST *Warm maroons and soft pinks maintain metal energy, as do curvy patterns and motifs. Brass and copper, soft metals, are more yin than iron or bronze, hard metals.*

THE FIREPLACE

A real fire provides Five-Element fire chi energy in its pure form, which enhances passion, excitement, spontaneity and brightness. Because of this, it is important, if possible, to position the fireplace in a location where it harmonizes with the Five-Element chi energy in that direction. The more yang

REMEDIES FOR UNFAVOURABLE LOCATIONS

THE NORTH Boost the overly quiet chi energy here by using brighter reds and maroons and by adding metal energy.

THE NORTH-EAST Calm the unsettling chi energy here using sombre reds and more yin surfaces – matt textures, carpets and tapestries.

THE NORTH-WEST Boost the over-serious chi energy here by using yellow fabrics, and by adding soil energy and soft metals such as copper or brass.

THE EAST Calm the over-active chi energy here by using yin pastel greens and yin materials like bamboo.

warmth of a fire is best suited to the northern part of a building where the usual energy is colder and more yin. On the northern side of the home, the Five-Element chi energy that is most in harmony with fire energy is the soil energy of the north-east. Therefore north-east from the centre of a building or room is the most suitable position.

Of the other positions, east, south-east and south-west are also harmonious in terms of the Five Elements. But being on the more yang sunny side of the home, they are less helpful in other respects. Avoid placing a fire in the south of the building as this could concentrate too much fire energy in one place and increase the risk of a fire.

Where the fireplace is in a favourable position, you can reflect more fire chi energy back into the room by hanging a mirror above it. Fire chi energy also can be introduced in the other forms – lighted candles, lanterns, oil lamps and bright lights, for example. Place them in dark corners where the chi energy is passive. If lights and lamps are impractical, shapes, colours and patterns associated with fire chi energy can be used in the interior decoration. Sharp, pointed or jagged shapes – stars, zigzags, triangles, pyramids – and hot yang colours such as yellows, oranges, reds and purples used in furnishing fabrics or wall coverings will add welcome fire-energy warmth to the room.

Since fire energy is supported by tree energy, tall plants will also help. You can also use a pointed fire-shaped plant, such as a yucca, or purple or red flowers.

ARRANGING SEATING AREAS

A living room is likely to be used by several people at a time, so the seating should be arranged to enhance a good sociable atmosphere. Often, if there is an uncomfortable atmosphere in the room, it can be attributed to an unsuccessful arrangement of the chairs and sofas. One general guideline is to have several items of seating (rather than one sofa, for example), and position them so that they all face the centre of the room. This also provides a variety of positions and directions appropriate to the varying needs and desires of your family and friends, and it should be possible for most people to find a direction that suits them. Ideally, wherever you are seated, most of the room will be in front of you. This is particularly important for parents of a household.

Positions and directions are most practical when you sit with your back against the wall facing the direction from which you want to benefit. For instance, if facing north is recommended, sit in the south facing the north. As well as rooms, apply this to your home as a whole.

Ideally, arrange seating so that it forms a balanced shape, such as a circle, square or octagon. If necessary, use items like side tables and plants to complete the shapes. Avoid placing chairs or sofas with their

For family harmony
Place a sofa in the north-west facing south-east, with two chairs in front and opposite each other, in the north-east facing south-west and in the south-west facing north-east, and one chair in the south-east facing north-west.
Closing the circle of seating in this way makes it particularly harmonious.

N
▼

backs to windows or doors. Your back to a door is the least secure position, especially if people are constantly entering or leaving the room. If possible, place sofas with their backs to the wall. Make sure, too, that people sitting in chairs are not exposed to cutting chi. For this reason, do not place chairs in front of protruding corners or near sharp-cornered furniture such as coffee tables and sideboards – a solid object such as a sideboard would have a stronger effect than a narrow table top. Use bushy plants to absorb cutting chi directed at chairs and sofas, and avoid sitting below a heavy beam.

Avoiding cutting chi
Trail a bushy, round-leaved plant over the sharp corner of a shelf or side table, or cover it with a cloth to prevent cutting chi.

N

For being productive
Place two sofas opposite each other in the east facing west and the west facing east; and a chair in the north-facing south. This is a dynamic arrangement, good for meetings and getting things done.

For lively conversation
Place two sofas as described left, but place the chair in the north-west facing south-east. This is a more harmonious arrangement where the chair is in balance between the chi energies of the sofas, but is also a lively arrangement good for a social gathering.

the dining room

Given today's hectic lifestyles, the evening meal may be the only time of day a family can all be together. However small your home, it is important to set a side a special area, even if it cannot be an entire room, where you can sit and eat around a table. A successful dining room or dining area creates a pleasant atmosphere where everyone can relax, enjoy their food and take time to digest it properly. It helps, too, if the room is conducive to conversation and family harmony. The food is the focal point; the surroundings have a supporting role.

FOOD AND CHI ENERGY

The food we eat is a major influence on our health. In Chinese medicine food is often an integral part of the treatment. Different foods have their own flow of chi energy. When you eat you take in not only the physical nutrients but also the chi energy of the food, which is a vital ingredient in the healing process.

The chi energy of food is easily influenced by the ambient chi energy, so it is essential that the chi energy in a dining room be conducive to good health. Nowadays we all recognise the importance of healthy eating, but we do not always get maximum benefit from our food, not simply because of what we eat, but how we eat it. It is much more healthy to sit down while eating, for example, than to eat on the run. This helps the stomach adopt a shape that is more conducive to proper digestion. Relax and take your time while eating. When you are tense and rushed, you secrete more acids in your stomach, which can lead to indigestion. It also helps to keep conversations at the table positive and enjoyable.

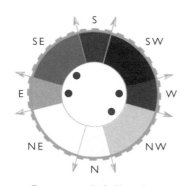

Recommended directions for a dining room
East, south-east, west and north-west of the centre of your home are all good directions.

FAVOURABLE LOCATIONS

East has a more lively atmosphere, and is a particularly good location for breakfasts because the sun shines on the eastern side of your home in the morning. The energy in the south-east favours conversation, and the west contains the chi energy that is best for pleasure, romance and entertainment. It is a particularly good location for the evening meal as the setting sun naturally energizes this part of your home. The north-west is best for more formal or more serious occasions. Eating north-east from the centre of your home exposes you to a sharp, piercing chi energy that is quick-changing and direct. This is not the ideal atmosphere for a relaxing meal.

USING COLOUR AND PATTERN

Check the direction of the dining room from the centre of your home. Use background colours and patterns that strengthen the chi energy of favourable directions, adding calming or enhancing features to fine-tune, depending on the ambience you aim to create. If it is a room used throughout the day, use bright colours. Darker shades work best in a dining room used mostly in the evenings.

The east is already vibrant and bright, and grassy greens can strengthen this. A leaf-patterned wallpaper or fabric with small touches of calming purple is ideal. In the gentler south-east use more sombre shades of green and blue. An irregular colour-washed finish is enhancing.

Warm pinks or even a dramatic rusty red on the walls in a western dining room is ideal for evening meals. To calm chi, colour-wash, rag-roll or sponge on paint. Soften it further with satin-finish cream paint on the woodwork. The north-west has dignity so plain painted walls in grey and white with touches of red and silver in accessories, and starched white table linen can enhance this in a formal dining room.

EAST *A green and white leaf-patterned fabric maintains tree energy here. Bright greens and blues are harmonious.*

SOUTH-EAST *Dark blues and greens maintain the energy here. Irregular-patterned wallpaper enhances chi energy.*

WEST *Strong dark reds work well in a dining room in this location.*

NORTH-WEST *The dignified chi energy here is maintained by grey and white. Silver accessories add to metal energy.*

matching tables with occasions

The yin and yang characteristics of materials and shapes make certain table tops more suited to some occasions than others.

Formal dinner parties
A more yin rectangle stretches energy and is more relaxing than a square top. Mahogany is more yang than softwoods, adding formality.

Family meals
An oval top spreads chi energy and is therefore more yin than a round top. A pine surface is also more yin and so particularly relaxing.

Business lunches
A square top is more yang and stimulating than a rectangular one. A hard marble top is also dynamic.

Romantic suppers
A round table is more yang and therefore more active than an oval one. A glass top adds excitement.

CHOOSING FURNISHINGS

The main aim in a dining area is to maintain the cleanliness required for handling food while promoting the relaxing atmosphere needed for good digestion and a convivial sociable ambience.

FURNITURE Easy-to-clean surfaces are essential. Wood is ideal since it does not speed up chi energy. Different woods affect chi energy differently (see above). To avoid poor digestion and discomfort, ensure sharp-cornered furniture is not directed at your guests.

LIGHTING Keep it flexible. Low lighting during dinner creates a romantic atmosphere, but at other times the rooom will require bright lighting. Lights which have dimmer switches will provide both these options. Candles add fire energy, which helps to produce a warm and vibrant atmosphere at the dining table.

WINDOW TREATMENTS   Fabric roller blinds are preferable to curtains since they prevent stagnation of chi energy.

FLOOR COVERINGS   Natural wood floors have a neutral effect on chi energy and are easy to clean. Rugs and carpets risk stagnation.

PAINTINGS   Choose images that provide a sympathetic backdrop to relaxed eating. Still lifes of food, convivial scenes or restful landscapes are all suitable. An attractive bowl of real fruit on a sideboard has a similar effect.

ACCESSORIES   A mirror on the wall or sideboard, reflecting the table, enhances the healthy chi energy produced by the food.

THE DINING TABLE

A round or square table is more yang and carries a dynamic kind of chi energy. An oval or rectangular table induces a more gentle energy, which is better for relaxed dining. Light softwoods, such as pine and elm, are more yin. Polished dark hardwoods, such as oak, mahogany and teak, are more yang. Hard surfaces, such as marble and glass, speed up the flow of chi energy across the table and make for a more stimulating, more exciting but also less relaxed atmosphere, which sometimes may be desirable. A linen table cloth will soften the atmosphere.

The combination of surface with shape allows you to influence the ambience of your dining area. You can combine more yin shapes (rectangles and ovals) with more yang materials and surfaces (marble, granite and glass), and more yang shapes (squares and circles) with more yin materials (light woods), or put yin materials and shapes together and yang materials and shapes together. All these combinations will create subtly different effects (see above left).

ENHANCING A MOOD WITH COLOUR

Relaxation | Stimulation | Vitality | Communication | Passion

Security | Romance | Formality | Warmth

table settings

Your choice of table linen, dishes and accessories has a powerful influence on the ambience around the dining table. Using the concepts of yin and yang (see page 10) you can design quite different settings, which affect the movement of chi energy across the table in a variety of ways.

The shape of the table and the material it is made of is also important (see page 42). Even minor details, such as a particular plant, a touch of strong bright colour in a table napkin or the shape of a place mat, all have subtle effects that contribute to the over-all atmosphere in the dining room.

Choosing appropriate settings for different occasions can make all the difference to the success of a meal, whether it be a formal social event or a casual everyday family affair.

Yin table setting
Soft yin surfaces and gentle colours create a more passive flow of chi energy. This results in a calmer, more relaxed ambience that is suitable for informal lunches or suppers and for easy-going everyday family meals.

Yang table setting
The exciting and stimulating chi energy that this creates is better suited to formal occasions. With the right touches, however, it can take on a romantic note. Yang settings are sparse and ordered with clean lines, strong colours and hard surfaces.

the bedroom

On average we spend six to nine hours out of every twenty-four in bed. Therefore the location and design of the bedroom and the positioning of the bed provide a superb opportunity to align yourself with the natural flow of energy in a way that helps you in other areas of your life.

A good night's sleep is essential for health, so it is also important to have a bedroom that calms you at the end of a busy day, and helps you to sleep well. It should also be a place where you wake up feeling refreshed, full of vitality and enthusiasm to make the most of a new day.

The bedroom has a significant influence on adult relationships, as it is where sex and physical intimacy take place. Privacy is also an important consideration. If possible, it is better not to use your bedroom for activities that require a different atmosphere, such as work. In the end, both will suffer.

FAVOURABLE LOCATIONS

Ideally, your bedroom should be exposed to sunlight at dawn which helps to increase your energy in the morning. If you have a choice of rooms, choose one where the atmosphere is calmest. The ideal direction for your bed is determined by what you are trying to achieve.

The north-west is ideal for parents. The chi energy here is more mature and can lead to greater responsibility, respect from others and improved ability to organize your life. The north has a quieter, more peaceful chi energy. This is particularly helpful for anyone who has difficulty sleeping. West is particularly favourable for romance, pleasure and content-

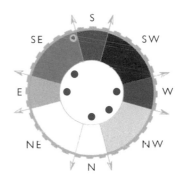

Recommended directions for an adult's bedroom
North, east, south-east, west and north-west of the centre of your home.

ment – desirable qualities in a bedroom shared by a couple. If your sex life has become dull, moving your bedroom to the north or west may bring increased or more satisfying sexual activity.

Generally, younger people benefit from a bedroom in the east or south-east of the home since they are building up their lives and the chi energy there favours making a good start.

an ideal bedroom

The chi energy of the west favours romance and contentment, making it an ideal location for a master bedroom. This position fulfils the requirements of promoting relaxation, restful sleep and the intimacy needed for romance.

Your bedroom should also contain lively, uplifting and cheerful elements to make it a pleasant place in which to wake up and begin the day. There is a playful aspect to the chi energy of the west which will produce this effect.

THINGS TO AVOID

SHARP CORNERS   Avoid spiky plants and rectangular or square furniture near the bed especially if it is directed at the bed.

MIRRORS   These reflect your own chi back at you while you sleep and impede the process of getting rid of old emotions. Cover or turn them to the wall at night.

HARD SHINY SURFACES
Glass, metal and marble all speed up chi energy and could prevent you from getting a good night's sleep.

EN SUITE BATHROOMS   These are not desirable because bathrooms introduce a heavier, damper atmosphere into bedrooms, and may drain them of healthy chi. Keep the door to an en suite bathroom closed, or screen the entrance with a curtain.

1 LIGHTING *Soft yin lighting is restful and intimate. Lampshades diffuse the harshness of electric light. Candles provide a more natural romantic glow and, if placed in the northeast, support soil energy.*

2 PLANTS *Round-leaved plants are soothing and, in the west or northwest of the room, help to maintain metal energy.*

3 STORAGE *Keep clothes and possessions tucked away in cupboards and wardrobes. Cupboards in alcoves or across entire walls reduce cutting chi.*

4 BED *A wood-framed bed has a neutral effect on chi energy. A headboard protects your head from fast flowing energy, though if your bed is against a wall this is less important. Place your bed in a favourable direction (see page 50). You should ideally be able to see the door and windows from your bed.*

5 BED LINEN *Use bed linen made of pure cotton, linen or silk. Pink shades and circular patterns support western chi energy. Do not leave beds unmade.*

6 FURNITURE *Bedroom furniture should have round edges. Sharp corners should not face the bed. Cutting chi directed at you while you sleep will disturb your chi energy and could affect your health.*

7 FLOOR COVERING *Soft yin materials slow chi energy and create a relaxing atmosphere. Fitted carpets are ideal in this room.*

8 WINDOW TREATMENT *Full draped or ruched curtains slow the flow of chi energy through windows at night and so promote restful sleep.*

9 WALL COVERING *Pastel colours are more yin and calming. Pink is harmonious in the west.*

10 PAINTINGS *Avoid reflective yang surfaces. Tapestries or pictures without glass are helpful. Placing pictures, candles and table lamps in pairs symbolizes intimacy.*

CHOOSING THE DECOR

In a western room the decor should support the metal chi energy there, which is favourable for a bedroom. Strengthen it using pinks, white and grey, and increase it with touches of red, silver and gold. More red increases the romantic ambience, and more yin pastel shades, or off-white or cream, creates peace and tranquillity. Rounded patterns on fabrics and wall-paper also maintain metal energy. Irregular patterns produced by sponging and colour-washing are calming if you have trouble sleeping.

DECOR FOR OTHER FAVOURABLE LOCATIONS

THE NORTH This chi energy fosters introspection and spirituality, favouring older people and those suffering from insomnia. However, it's not so good for young people. Depending on your situation, strengthen the naturally cool chi energy using cream and off-white, or enhance it with warmer pinks and reds.

THE NORTH-WEST This natural ambience is responsible and serious, but again, too sombre for younger people. To strengthen it use grey, white and pink. Check patterns which incorporate some yellow, brown or black add soil energy to support the metal energy here.

EAST AND SOUTH-EAST Both these locations are better for younger people since they are generally stimulating and lively, especially in the mornings where they are exposed to the rising sun. Use more yin middle or pastel shades of green or blue and irregular patterns to calm the atmosphere for sleeping.

NORTH *Warm pink, burgundy or red increases vitality in an otherwise quiet and reflective bedroom in this direction.*

NORTH-WEST *Grey, white and pink strengthen the natural sombre energy in this location.*

EAST AND SOUTH-EAST *Blues and greens help to strengthen active tree energy in both these locations.*

THE BED

The right bed can revitalize your energy, influence aspects of your everyday life and, indeed, shape your destiny.

Wood is the most favourable material for the bed frame because, unlike metal, it does not alter the local magnetic field. Wood also has a more subtle influence on the movement of chi energy. Bed frames made of brass and cast iron speed up chi energy, which is not generally conducive to restful sleep. Water beds are not recommended as they produce a damp, heavy atmosphere, which can lead to feelings of stagnation.

REMEDIES FOR UNFAVOURABLE LOCATIONS

THE NORTH-EAST Calm the sharp, piercing chi energy here by using pale yellows or rusty colours rather than bright shades of red and pink. Add calming metal energy with more yin curved, rather than more yang circular, patterns or objects.

THE SOUTH Calm the excessively passionate chi energy in this location by using pale yin shades of purple and the soil colours yellow and black. Soft matt textures, such as those on carpets,

tapestries and upholstered furniture, will also help. Add soil energy by using check patterns, low spreading plants in unglazed terracotta pots or unglazed clay sculptures.

THE SOUTH-WEST Stimulate the settled chi energy here using bright yellows and browns with touches of rich purple. Adding metal energy in its more yin forms – bronze and copper will provide more stability.

Keep the space beneath your bed empty to avoid chi energy stagnating under you while you sleep. If you store things under your bed, clear it out and clean there regularly.

Choose a mattress made of natural materials. Cotton, wool, straw and hair are preferable to foam and other synthetics, which carry a static charge that can make you feel drained of physical and emotional energy. Pocket-sprung mattresses contain metal springs which affect the local magnetic field and cause the movement of chi energy to become chaotic. This can make you feel confused and disorientated.

Futons are ideal beds in Feng Shui terms. They are made of four to eight layers of thick cotton wadding bound by a strong cotton cover. In Japan they are placed on the floor on bamboo tatami mats, but in the West most people use wooden bases to raise them off the floor so that they can be aired properly.

Since they are used next to your skin, it is even more important that sheets, pillowcases, blankets and duvet covers are made of pure cotton, linen, silk or wool. Cotton and linen are preferable because they 'breathe' better than silk. Avoid synthetic fabrics. Quilts and duvets, likewise, should contain only natural down or cotton filling. Keep bed linen and bedcovers raised well above the floor, so that air can circulate freely under the bed. All bedding should be regularly washed and also well aired, preferably outside.

directions for your bed

The choice of rooms may be limited, but the position of your bed is often more flexible. The direction you sleep in affects your whole life as well as how well you sleep. Ideally, place your bed along an axis that passes through the centre of your home, and so that your head will point in a helpful direction.

Head pointing **North**	This quiet direction can help with insomnia, but can also make your whole life too quiet. It is beneficial for elderly people, enhancing feelings of peace, tranquillity and spirituality, as well as for babies who wake often.
Head pointing **North-East**	This direction is too sharp and piercing for good sleep. It can make you feel on edge and increase violent nightmares. It may improve your motivation but it is inadvisable to sleep like this over a long period.
Head pointing **East**	This is ideal for young people, making them feel that everything is ahead of them and that anything can happen. Good for career-building, ambition and getting things done, it is also ideal for growth and for making life busier.
Head pointing **South-East**	Good communication and increased creativity are the benefits you can expect from sleeping in this direction. It encourages growth and a more active life, but in a more subtle way than the east.
Head pointing **South**	Its high energy and hot fiery nature means this direction is not conducive to sound sleep. It can also lead to heated arguments with the possible risk of separation. Although passion enhancing, use it only in the short term.
Head pointing **South-West**	This is a settled position which implies more peaceful relationships, but it can make you too cautious. It also means you sleep with your feet pointing north-east and the north-east/south-west axis can make your life unstable.
Head pointing **West**	This provides good sleep and general contentment, and may even improve income and romance. However, contentment can lead to laziness and low motivation so the west is more suitable for those in established careers.
Head pointing **North-West**	This direction is associated with leadership and feeling in control. It promotes longer, deeper sleep and is suited to older people with the experience to exercise authority wisely. Recommended for parents.

the children's room

This often has to function as a bedroom and playroom, so the challenge is to make it fun during the day and peaceful at night. Balancing these two considerations will affect your choice of location, the direction in which you place the bed or beds, the furnishing and decor. For many parents the ideal children's bedroom is one where they sleep soundly the whole night through, but the chi energy in the room must also be supportive of activity, stimulation and other needs of growing children.

Sometimes two or more children may have to share a room and this can lead to friction If you place all the beds in the same direction, it can make relations between the children more harmonious.

FAVOURABLE LOCATIONS

Ideally, your children's bedroom should be exposed to energizing sunlight at dawn. This would be the case in the east and south-east of your home. The west, which receives sun in the evening, is also favourable, especially for children who tend to be hyperactive.

The east contains the youthful uplifting chi energy associated with growth and development. This chi energy is also stimulating and active and represents the rising sun, which symbolizes the future. It has the feeling of the beginning of a new day, just as a child is at the beginning of a new life. Achieving restful sleep could be a problem, however, as eastern chi energy may be too active, and you may need to take steps to calm it (see pages 52–53).

Bedrooms in the south-east can also promote growth and lively activity. But the chi energy here is gentler than in the east, and could encourage a more harmonious development in life. It is also a more soothing place for sleeping.

The west carries a more settled chi energy and would be the best location for a peaceful night's sleep. The chi energy here is playful, but does not convey the same benefits as the other directions in terms of a child's harmonious growth and development.

Recommended directions for a child's bedroom
East, south-east, and west of the centre of your home.

a child's ideal bedroom

The chi energy of the east is ideal for a growing child, being bright, positive, forward-looking and active. It also encourages imaginative play and healthy mental development.

At the same time, good rest is vital for a child, so the liveliness of the east may need to be moderated. Balance the need for stimulation with a peaceful environment that promotes good sleep.

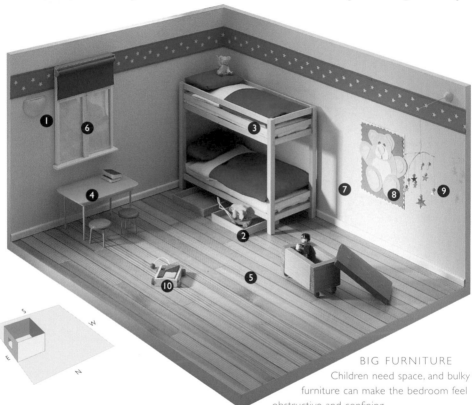

THINGS TO AVOID

OPEN DOORS Keep the bedroom door closed at night and draw the curtains. This calms the flow of energy and helps children fall asleep more easily.

BEDHEADS BELOW WINDOWS Do not place bedheads under windows as the chi energy here is more active and may prevent a good night's sleep.

BIG FURNITURE Children need space, and bulky furniture can make the bedroom feel obstructive and confining.

CLUTTER It is easy for children's rooms to become littered with their possessions, ultimately becoming confusing and frustrating. Encourage children to keep their rooms tidy and to get rid of outgrown items.

ELECTRICAL EQUIPMENT To reduce unnecessary electrical radiation, do not have TVs, video machines and personal computers in children's bedrooms.

❶ LIGHTING *Uplights that reflect off the ceiling support tree energy. To avoid trailing flexes, use wall lights instead of lamps.*

❷ STORAGE *Lots of units help clear the room for play. Place them within reach so children can put away their own toys. Floor boxes are ideal.*

❸ BEDS *Bunk beds save space and allow children to sleep in the same direction – helpful if they squabble. If your baby is not sleeping, place the cot so that the baby's head is pointing north. Beds should be cosy and inviting so use plump pillows and fluffy duvets in natural fibres. Blue is a particularly harmonious colour in this direction.*

❹ FURNITURE *Rounded stools and tables prevent cutting chi. When they sit at the table in the east of the room children face east, intensifying active chi energy. Bright colours are stimulating.*

❺ FLOOR COVERING *Natural wood supports tree energy, reduces stagnation and is easy to clean.*

❻ WINDOWS *Fabric blinds slow chi energy through the windows without causing stagnation. When rolled up, they expose the window completely, maximizing the room's exposure to favourable chi.*

❼ WALLS *Soft shades of blue are calming. Star patterns adds fire energy.*

❽ PAINTINGS *Fabric wall-hangings are good as they slow chi energy. Choose positive images to suit your children's needs. Bright colours like red, yellow and orange, are more yang and stimulating. Soft colours, like blues and greens, are more yin and soothing.*

❾ MOBILE *Mobiles can be arousing or relaxing. A shiny metal mobile in the west of the room is more yang whereas a soft fabric mobile in pastel colours is more yin and peaceful. Do not hang mobiles directly over a child's bed.*

❿ TOYS *Wooden toys are strong and durable, yet warm and pleasing to touch. Put toys away at night to calm chi energy.*

CHOOSING THE DECOR

Maintain the favourable active tree chi energy by using harmonious blue as a background colour but in softer, more yin shades to introduce calm. Elsewhere in the room, bright greens, yellows and blues in smaller quantities will also be harmonious, yet stimulating. Plain walls and bed covers are more yang and help to reduce any impression of clutter. Yellow is harmonious in any direction. Star motifs introduce fire energy and are calming to the tree energy of the east. For greater calm, use soft yin pastel shades and bring in more pale purple.

REMEDIES FOR UNFAVOURABLE LOCATIONS

THE NORTH   Boost the quiet chi energy of this direction by using bright red colours, shiny metal mobiles and metal wind chimes.

THE NORTH-EAST   Calm this sharp chi energy with more yin soil and metal energies: rusty pinks, pale yellow and generous use of fabrics and other soft matt surfaces. Place a cloth mobile in a harmonious colour in the north-east of the room.

THE SOUTH   Calm this hyperactive chi energy by adding yin soil energy. Remedies as suggested for the north-east are good, but use pale yellow and buff rather than pink. Place a terracotta bowl containing charcoal under the bed.

THE SOUTH-WEST   Boost this over-mature chi by adding more yang fire and metal energies: purples, reds and pinks in zigzag or circular patterns.

THE NORTH-WEST   Calm the over-solemn chi energy found here by adding water chi energy: creamy colours and irregularly patterned walls.

DECOR FOR OTHER FAVOURABLE LOCATIONS

THE SOUTH-EAST   This location shares many characteristics with the east, but is gentler and therefore unnecessary to introduce so many calming devices in this direction. Strengthening the natural ambience should be sufficient. Use stronger shades of the harmonious colours – greens and blues – while keeping them bright and cheerful, rather than sombre. Patterns with a vertical motif are also appropriate here.

THE WEST   This has a settled, contented ambience which could well suit an anxious or overactive child, or when children are going through a squabbling phase. But if you need to introduce a more stimulating, energizing quality to the room, use yang shades of red and pink, together with touches of bright yellow. Check patterns will also help.

SOUTH-EAST
Vertically striped patterns of harmonious green and blue will maintain the buoyant energy of a room in this location.

WEST *The metal energy of this direction can be enhanced with yang shades of red, pink and bright yellow in check patterns.*

the kitchen

Food has special significance in the Far East because it is widely used for healing. Practitioners of Japanese and Chinese medicine believe that a healthy well-balanced diet leads to good health and longevity. Air, water and food provide not only life-sustaining nutrients, but each also has its own flow of chi energy. There is relatively little we can do about the air we breathe, but we have more choice about drinking water and a much greater choice over the food we eat and how it's prepared. How we exercise those choices has a direct influence on our health and well-being.

Food preparation is influenced by the surrounding chi energy, so having kitchens in a favourable location is vital. Since kitchens combine the incompatible elements of fire and water, the location must be one where these elements can be harmonized, and particular consideration must be given to positioning the stove and sink (see page 58).

FAVOURABLE LOCATIONS

The most suitable positions are to the east and south-east of the centre of your home, where the energy is bright, uplifting and supportive to growth, activity and development. Also, the Five-Element tree energy of the east and south-east is compatible with both water and fire. The resulting harmonious flow of energy through the kitchen benefits the movement of chi energy throughout the home. The early morning sun warms and energizes the east and south-east sides of the home, making them particularly good locations for kitchens that double as breakfast rooms.

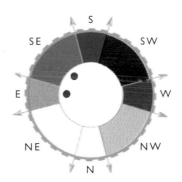

Recommended directions for your kitchen
East and south-east of the centre of your home.

Certain locations should be avoided if possible. The cold and quick-changing north-eastern energy is not the best atmosphere for creating healthy well-balanced meals. The quiet and still northern energy does not have sufficient vitality to promote good health. The south is also undesirable as it is in the position of Five-Element fire energy. Too much fire energy in one place can produce unbalanced meals and increase the risk of house fires.

USING COLOUR AND PATTERN

Enhance the favourable chi energy in an eastern or south-eastern kitchen by using off-white or cream as the main colours, with bright green in the east and dark greens and blues in the south-east used as accents. The chi energy in these locations will be boosted by irregular patterns, whether in decorative paint finishes on walls and woodwork, or in a wallpaper or fabric with a figurative motif. An all-over leaf pattern maintains tree energy here; or choose a culinary theme such as vegetables or fruits. Watery subjects in harmonious blues are also appropriate because Five-Element water energy is supportive to tree energy.

CHOOSING FURNISHINGS

Kitchens should be bright, clean and dry, as this will have a positive influence on the chi energy of your food before you eat it.

PLANTS   Place healthy leafy plants between the stove and sink to harmonize fire and water.

LIGHTING   Natural light is ideal; complement it with spotlights directed at the corners. Encourage sunlight to enter the room to help create an uplifting atmosphere. Sunlight also helps keep a kitchen dry, and therefore the chi energy fresh and clean.

FOOD AND FLOWERS   Displays of fresh foods and flowers promote a healthy flow of chi energy.

FURNITURE   Wood is the ideal surface for food preparation. Stainless steel and shiny ceramic tiles create a more yang, fast-moving atmosphere, but this may become a problem if you tend to spend a large amount of time in the kitchen. Laminates and vinyl tiles tend to block chi energy. Fit cupboards, shelves and worktops with rounded corners and edges to avoid cutting chi.

MATERIALS *Shiny ceramic tiles help keep chi energy moving and prevent stagnation. Cork flooring is more yin, enabling you to spend lots of time comfortably in the kitchen.*

COLOURS *Blues and greens maintain tree energy in the east and south-east. Touches of purple are enhancing and yellow is harmonious in all directions.*

MOTIFS *Images of fruit and vegetables in harmonious colours are sympathetic in a kitchen.*

FLOORS   Natural wood flooring is recommended, because it is practical, warm and easy to clean. Cork tiles are the most yin wooden flooring you can have in a kitchen.

STORAGE   Do not allow the kitchen to become cluttered with appliances, gadgets and utensils. These can cause stagnation, resulting in harmful influences on food preparation. Have well-arranged storage space and keep surfaces clean and tidy. Wash down open shelves and clear out cupboards regularly.

THE STOVE

In Feng Shui terms, the stove represents the creation of life because the food prepared on it contributes to the creation of life in your body. It is the most important appliance in the kitchen and should be as large as space permits. If your stove is positioned against a wall, hang a mirror on the wall above it. This will visually double its size, thus enhancing the life-creating image. You will also be able to see what is happening behind you when you are cooking.

Stoves with a natural flame are preferable to electric ones. Gas is ideal, but wood- or coal-burning stoves are good alternatives. A natural flame stove, like a real fire, also adds to the comfortable atmosphere of the room. Avoid electric stoves where possible as these give off electromagnetic fields which can negatively affect the chi energy of your food, and consequently your health. Microwaves are also not recommended. Work surfaces must be easy to clean and stainless steel is the best choice for a stove top.

A stove on an island in the kitchen will allow you to face into the room while you are cooking and to see the windows and doors. It also gives you a greater choice of positions within the kitchen so that you can face the direction most favourable to you. Facing into the room also makes for a more sociable setting as you can see and talk to your friends and family while you are cooking for them.

Adding metal and soil energies
The effects of kitchens located in unfavourable positions (see page 58) can be eased by adding soil energy or metal energy. Displaying clay pots or stainless steel pans is an appropriate means of doing this.

positioning the stove and sink

The stove and sink represent fire and water Five-element energy so should not be placed next to each other. Try to ensure that the stove and sink are in locations where Five-Element chi energy is compatible (see below). If possible, keep refrigerators and washing machines away from the stove.

DIRECTION/EFFECTS	SOLUTION
NORTH Unfavourable. The chi energy here is too quiet to promote health and vitality.	Add more metal chi energy. Stainless steel surfaces, saucepans and other objects that are round or made of metal will help. Red, white and silver are helpful colours. Add plants.
NORTH-EAST Unfavourable. This direction is on an unstable axis, making it too unpredictable and disorientating.	To stabilize chi energy, place small china bowls filled with sea salt in the south-west and north-east corners. Add metal chi energy.
EAST Favourable. Fire and water mix harmoniously with eastern tree chi energy, so this location is beneficial for both stove and sink. The chi energy here helps prevent possible stagnation in damp areas.	
SOUTH-EAST Favourable. The tree chi energy here is harmonious with fire and water chi energies. Although not as active as in the east, it is enough to avoid stagnation.	
SOUTH Unfavourable. The fire chi energy here makes this unfavourable for stoves as too much fire energy would be concentrated in one place, increasing the risk of accidental fires.	Add more soil energy: low, flat things made of clay or charcoal in a low clay pot next to the stove. Black and yellow are helpful colours. Place plants near the sink.
SOUTH-WEST Unfavourable. This direction is on an unstable axis, making it too unpredictable and disorientating.	To stabilize chi energy, place small china bowls filled with sea salt in the south-west and north-east corners. Add metal chi energy.
WEST Unfavourable. In this direction metal energy clashes with the fire energy of the stove, and is drained by the water energy of the sink.	Add more soil energy (charcoal in a low clay pot) near the stove, and metal energy (white flowers in a metal pot) next to the sink.
NORTH-WEST Unfavourable. In this direction metal energy clashes with the fire energy of the stove, and is drained by the water energy of the sink.	Add more soil energy (charcoal in a low clay pot) near the stove, and metal energy (white flowers in a metal pot) next to the sink.

the bathroom

Water is the main element in the bathroom. Rooms with a lot of water tend to have damp, wet surfaces and more humid atmospheres than other rooms. This can lead to a heavier flow of chi energy, which makes the room prone to stagnation. The situation is particularly risky when there is little or no exposure to sunlight and fresh air, so internal bathrooms without windows are the least desirable.

Bathrooms are often tucked away in small spaces in a home, but large bathrooms are preferable since it is easier to avoid a harmful build-up of stagnant chi energy if there is plenty of space. En suite bathrooms, linked to bedrooms, are undesirable in Feng Shui terms.

FAVOURABLE LOCATIONS

The activities which take place in bathrooms all involve Five-Element water chi energy in its pure form, so you need to allocate them carefully. Another consideration is the draining effect of the bath, shower and toilet. These functions make it difficult to allocate bathrooms in positions that are helpful to the flow of chi energy in the home generally. If they are in unfavourable locations, they can have a harmful draining effect on chi energy in the rest of your home. If you have a choice in the matter, it is best not to allocate your bathroom opposite the main door of your house, near staircases or near the dining room or kitchen.

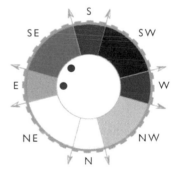

Recommended directions for a bathroom
East and south-east of the centre of your home.

Water is supportive to the Five-Element tree chi energy of the east and south-east and, as long as there are plenty of windows, this is also often a sunny part of the house, which helps to keep the room dry. The dryness and the exposure to sunlight are also both helpful in preventing stagnation.

The least desirable location is in the north-east of your home, which should be avoided if at all possible. Other locations all risk varying consequences for your physical and mental health. Use Five-Element solutions to mitigate the negative effects (see page 62).

USING COLOUR AND PATTERN

Enhance the vibrant chi energy in favourable east and south-east locations by using mainly cream and off-white in the paintwork and bathroom fittings. Use bright green in the east and dark blues and greens in the south-east in accessories such as towels, bath mats and blinds. Plain finishes on the walls are more yang, which is helpful here, but irregular patterns support water energy and would be enhancing. Employ them in moisture-resistant paint finishes, rather than fabrics or wallpaper. More yang materials (see below) are also beneficial. Colour and pattern can also be used to mitigate the effects of unfavourable bathroom locations. See page 62 for specific solutions.

COLOURS *Green and blue used in bathroom accessories support tree energy in the east and south-east.*

CHOOSING FURNISHINGS

The main objectives in a bathroom are to keep the room bright, dry and fresh and to counteract the tendency for chi energy to stagnate in humid conditions. Good ventilation dispels humid-ity and helps to prevent stagnation. Open the window and let in plenty of fresh air every day. This is preferable to using electric extractor fans.

MATERIALS *Hard, smooth and reflective materials used on floors, walls and other surfaces speed up the flow of chi energy, which helps to reduce the risk of stagnation in humid bathrooms.*

LIGHTING   Natural light is best. A bright sunny room creates a lively dry atmosphere and sunlight charges up chi energy and helps stimulate its flow. If natural light is limited, keep the room well lit, especially the corners.

WINDOW TREATMENTS   Slatted blinds are a good compromise between the needs of privacy and those of light. Avoid thick curtains. Keep blinds or curtains open as much as possible.

PLANTS   Plenty of leafy plants make the room feel fresh and alive and minimize the risk of chi energy stagnating in corners. Plants also help to absorb the extra humidity in steamy bathrooms, and generally grow well there for that reason.

FURNITURE Keep furniture and bric-a-brac to a minimum. Too many objects in the bathroom create a damper, more stagnant atmosphere. In particular, avoid overuse of fabrics. Surfaces should be easy to keep clean and dry. Hard shiny surfaces such as chrome, glazed ceramic tiles, polished marble and glass are more yang and stimulate the flow of chi energy, thereby counteracting stagnation.

MIRRORS Mirrors speed up the flow of chi energy, which is a positive feature in a bathroom where you are striving to avoid stagnation. Since bathrooms are often small, mirrors can also give a feeling of space. But do not have mirrors facing each other (see page 90).

THE TOILET

The toilet should be as inconspicuous as possible. To minimize its draining and flushing effect on the chi energy of the rest of the home, position it well away from the bathroom door if possible. If the bathroom is large enough, site it so that it cannot be seen from the door, and make sure it is not reflected in any mirrors. Ideally, place the toilet in the east or south-east of the room, concealed behind a half wall, screen or curtain. Keep the toilet lid closed as much as possible, but especially while it is being flushed. Keep the bathroom door closed, especially if it is an en suite bathroom.

THE BATHROOM FLOOR

Natural wooden flooring is neutral in its effect on the flow of chi energy, and helps to support tree energy, which is particularly advantageous in bathrooms in the east, south-east and south. Avoid synthetic materials such as carpets, rugs and linoleum. Marble, granite, glass and other hard, smooth, more yang surfaces speed up the flow of chi energy, especially if they are shiny and reflective, creating a much more exciting, stimulating environment and one that helps avoid stagnation.

Stone and ceramic tiles have similar properties to marble, but if the floor is uneven they tend to scatter the energy. This can be an advantage in locations to the north, where there is a particularly high risk of energy stagnating throughout the entire room, and such floors are especially desirable if the bathroom has little exposure to natural light.

solutions for bathrooms

Counteract the detrimental effect of unfavourable locations by harmonizing the bathroom's water chi energy with Five-Element chi energy in the relevant location. Determine the direction of the bathroom, then consult the chart below. Eight Direction colours (see page 74) are also helpful.

DIRECTION/EFFECTS	SOLUTION
NORTH Unfavourable. The bathroom's water energy added to water energy of the north is overwhelming. The chi energy here is quiet and still, risking stagnation. This can deplete your vitality and make you too introverted.	Grow tall plants to introduce tree energy and drain water energy. They will also absorb humidity and produce oxygen.
NORTH-EAST Unfavourable. This least desirable location can cause unpredictable life changes and possible ill-health.	Place sea salt in a white china bowl in the north-east area.
EAST Favourable. Water chi energy is harmonious with the tree chi energy found in this direction. However, the downward movement of a toilet being flushed and bath water being drained is contrary to a tree's upward movement.	Increase the upward tree energy by growing tall plants in the bathroom. Wooden floors and fittings will also help.
SOUTH-EAST Favourable. The effects of a bathroom in this direction are similar to those of a bathroom in the east, where water draining away may limit the upward tree movement.	Increase the upward tree energy by growing tall plants in the bathroom. Wooden floors and fittings will also help.
SOUTH Unfavourable. Water chi energy destroys the fire chi energy here. This can lead to lack of passion, fewer opportunities to achieve recognition, and vulnerability to law suits.	Harmonize water and fire by growing tall plants and have wooden and green accessories.
SOUTH-WEST Unfavourable. This chi energy is unstable and the soil energy of the south-west is destructive to water chi energy. If unchecked this location can compromise your health.	Boost metal energy by placing a small bowl of sea salt in the bathroom along with iron pots.
WEST Unfavourable. The metal chi energy of this direction is drained by water energy, which could cause a draining effect on your ability to increase your income.	Boost metal chi energy by growing red-flowering plants in iron pots.
NORTH-WEST Unfavourable. Water energy drains metal chi energy, maybe leading to feeling disorganized and out of control.	Build up metal chi energy by growing white-flowering plants.

the home office

Working from home has many advantages. Not only are you able to set the pace of what you do and the way you do it, but you also have a greater measure of control over your working environment. You can choose where you sit, the kind of lighting that suits you, the shape of your desk and so on. This gives you the opportunity to design your office to enhance your productivity and effectiveness, so that you can achieve the success you are seeking. Everything in the room should be working for you, not against you.

One of the challenges with a modern home office, studio or work-room is to balance electrical radiation from the various pieces of electronic equipment with more natural chi energy. The positioning of your desk and chair in relation to computers, printers, telephones, fax machines and copiers, as well as their direction in the room are vitally important (see pages 65 and 68).

FAVOURABLE LOCATIONS

Each has particular advantages which could be helpful, depending on the type of business you are engaged in, or the stage of your career.

The east has the chi energy to help you become busier, more active, more focussed and better able to put your good ideas into practice. This is the best position if you are starting a new business or embarking on a new career. The chi energy in the south-east is similar but gentler, which is more helpful for communication and the harmonious development and growth of your business.

The fiery chi energy in the south will help you attract attention for your business, and is more likely to lead to widespread acclaim and recognition for your work. If success is related to you being in the public eye, this is the place for your office.

The north-west is ideal for leadership, organization and for inspiring and maintaining the respect of others – qualities that would be helpful if you are working with, or perhaps directing, a team of people.

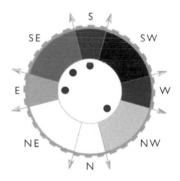

Recommended directions for a home office
East, south-east, south and north-west of the centre of your home.

EAST AND SOUTH-EAST *Vertical stripes support helpful forward-looking chi energy here. Blue and green are also supportive colours.*

SOUTH *The colour purple maintains the fire chi energy here, which helps you achieve success and greater public recognition for your work.*

NORTH-WEST *This metal energy that is conducive to organization is enhanced by soil energy, so greys and whites with bits of yellow are helpful.*

CHOOSING FURNISHINGS

The ideal atmosphere in an office is stimulating, but not stressful. Because you may work there for long periods at a time, choose furnishings that tend to be more yang, but balance them with restful more yin elements.

FURNITURE   The desk is the most important item (see opposite). The desk chair should keep you alert while working, but not strain you physically or mentally. Much office furniture – filing cabinets, shelving systems – has sharp corners. Where it is impossible to find rounded alternatives, soften the edges with plants.

LIGHTING   Natural is better than artificial so choose a room with large windows. Avoid fluorescent lighting.

PLANTS   Plenty of leafy plants in the room balance electrical radiation. A peace lily is particularly helpful.

STORAGE   Work generates a great deal of paraphernalia – papers, files, books and so on. Have plenty of storage so that you can keep papers neat and well-organized, and avoid the stagnating chi associated with clutter. Cupboards are preferable to open bookshelves.

USING COLOUR AND PATTERN

Check the direction of your office from the centre of your home. Aim to main the chi energy of favourable directions, adding enhancing or calming touches. Use paler yin shades and more subtle patterns to reduce the stress in an over-active office. Where the chi energy is too unstimulating for productive work, use brighter, stronger colours.

In the east the chi energy is busy and active; vertical stripes in bright and dark greens maintain this helpful ambience. The gentler south-east direction can take enhancing colours; match blues or greens with cream and off-white on more yang plain walls. The chi energy in the hotter south will be maintained with middle shades of purple; soften it slightly with black and white touches. The north-west of your home is a more serious direction and is particularly appropriate to a more formal, businesslike working atmosphere; try grey, white and maroon with touches of yellow. Check patterns are also suitable here, because they add soil energy which supports the metal energy of the north-west.

THE DESK

Your desk and its accessories (see page 66–67) both influence how productively you work. A large desk helps you to feel dignified and powerful. It also conveys the impression that you have room to expand. A small cramped desk can make you feel constrained, and that you have nowhere further to go. A round or oval desk is usually preferable to a square or rectangular one. It is more relaxing to work at for long periods of time, and avoids the risk of cutting chi from sharp corners.

A wooden desk promotes a natural flow of chi energy, making you feel more at ease in your room. More yin softwoods like pine give a relaxed casual feel; darker hardwoods like teak and mahogany add formality. Glass is a stimulating surface for a desk, but is not as suitable as wood for lengthy working sessions.

Ideally, you should situate your desk in a beneficial location, facing a helpful direction, looking into the room, and being able to see the doors and windows easily. Avoid sitting next to electrical equipment, which can lead to reduced concentration and ill-health. Try to minimize your exposure to synthetic materials that emit toxic fumes.

In some cases your own needs may not be the only consideration. If several people use your home office and work as a team, arrange the chairs to enhance harmony between them. Generally, it is best to place the desks so that the people sitting in them face the centre of the room.

If your work involves having business meetings at home, arrange the chairs in your home office so that your visitors feel positive about working with you. If your office is large enough, set up a special area for meetings. Each direction has specific characteristics which promote certain qualities in the people sitting in those positions. You can use this knowledge to seat people appropriately, depending on their own personal and professional characteristics, and on what you are hoping to achieve from your meeting.

the desk top

The chi energy of your working environment is affected not only by your desk itself (see page 65), but also by the way you arrange the tools of your trade on the top. Favourable positioning can make the difference between a productive, creative and inspiring atmosphere that helps you achieve your goals, and one that is frustrating and demotivating.

To make your desktop work for you, first determine the directions on it: place it in your chosen location in the room, then find the centre, establish magnetic north and place a grid of the Eight Directions over it. Place objects in sectors where they harmonize with the energy of that direction (see right). Clutter obstructs the harmonious flow of chi energy so keep papers and paraphernalia neatly organized in convenient drawers and filing cabinets.

NORTH:TRANQUILLITY
Plants, especially peace lilies can help minimize the disturbing effects of electrical radiation from office equipment. They also bring their own living energy into the working situation.

NORTH-EAST:MOTIVATION
Put objects here that will encourage you to work harder. They could be material, such as a financial forecast or the prospect of making a good profit.

◀ N

NORTH-WEST: ORGANIZATION *Keep your diary, forward planner or organizer in this position.*

EAST: FUTURE DREAMS
*This is the place for a
reminder of what you can
achieve with hard work, such
as the car you've always
wanted.*

**SOUTH-EAST:
COMMUNICATION**
*This is the right
position for your mail
tray, the telephone and
fax if you have one.*

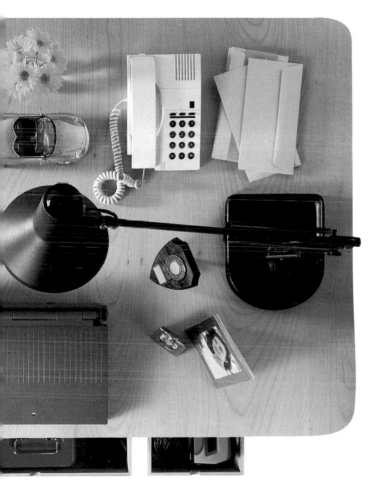

**SOUTH: PUBLIC
RECOGNITION**
*Keep things such as
awards, prizes or
other public accolades
in this direction.*

**SOUTH-WEST:
FAMILY
HARMONY**
*Photographs or other
mementoes of your
family are
appropriate here.*

WEST: FINANCE *This is the place for cheque
books, cashboxes and anything else to do with
money. If your chair is situated in the west, you
will be facing east, a favorable direction for
building up a career quickly.*

positioning your desk and chair

There are 64 possible positions for a desk and chair, each with a different mix of chi energies. The positions described below are some of the most advantageous. The position immerses you in the underlying flow of chi in the room. But the direction you face sitting at the desk has the greatest influence.

Sitting **N-W** Facing South-East	This is best for a chief executive or top manager. North-west enhances leadership, organization, responsibility, dignity and trustworthiness. Facing south-east is helpful for expansion, creativity and communication.
Sitting **N-E** Facing East	The motivating chi energy of the north-east combines with the active chi energy of the east, which is useful for someone lacking drive, or looking for a new direction. It is particularly suitable for people dealing in real estate.
Sitting **E** Facing East	Here the chi energy of the east is even more intense, favouring quick starts and fast growth. This is excellent for anyone starting a career or business, particularly in the computer or electronics industry.
Sitting **E** Facing South-East	This is similar to sitting east facing east, but less intense. Its qualities are conducive to communication, creativity and harmonious development. Media or travel business employees are likely to find this supportive.
Sitting **E** Facing South	This is helpful for putting ideas into practice, getting public recognition and promoting, so is suitable for PR, sales or advertising employees. However, it is not a good position if you feel restless and have difficulty concentrating.
Sitting **S-E** Facing East	This is similar to sitting east facing south-east, only the importance of the directions is reversed. The desk determines the underlying chi energy but the direction you face has greater influence, so east is dominant.
Sitting **S-E** Facing South	This combination of energies is ideal for people working in PR, marketing or communication. It is also good for lawyers. The chi energy is very active, so is not advisable for someone who becomes easily stressed or excited.
Sitting **W** Facing East	West chi energy relates to income, contentment and pleasure. Facing east helps you to become more ambitious, active and better able to put your ideas into practice. This is particularly helpful for people working in finance.

DESIGN ELEMENTS in FENG SHUI

Choose the objects you put in your home
carefully so that they encourage helpful
rather than unhelpful chi energy. Colours,
shapes, materials, plants, water and light,
among other things, all have implications
which can work for you or against you.

manipulating chi

No matter what it is, every object you place in your home influences the flow of chi energy. Some objects have powerful effects and others much weaker or neutral ones. Even the empty spaces, or lack of them, between objects or in rooms and hallways can help smooth the path of chi energy through your home or obstruct it. The more active design elements that help you to manipulate chi energy include water, lights, mirrors, plants, fresh flowers, crystals, candles, sounds and sea salt. Things such as furniture, carpets, curtains and cupboards are less potent. However, although relatively passive, your furniture sometimes defines where you will be in your home – your location and the direction you face. Its main function, therefore, should be to enable you to spend most of your time in the most favourable positions.

Generally, it is the shapes, colours and materials of furnishings and decorative objects that affect the flow of chi energy. The shape of an object physically alters the way chi energy flows around it, and how chi energy flows into and out of it. The colour determines the light frequencies reflected into the room, which will then influence the chi energy in that room. The materials that objects are made of also convey very different kinds of chi energy.

FENG SHUI GUIDELINES FOR CHOOSING FURNITURE

ONE	TWO	THREE	FOUR
FIVE ELEMENTS AND EIGHT DIRECTIONS Look at the Five Elements chart (page 18) and the Eight Directions colour wheel (page 74) to check that furniture will bring the type of chi energy you want in your life.	**HARMONIOUS COLOURS, SHAPES AND MATERIAL** Check the colours, patterns, shapes and materials charts on pages 73, 77 and 78 to ensure your piece will harmonize with its intended location in your home.	**YIN AND YANG** Consult the charts on pages 14 and 15 to decide which furniture will make the chi energy in your home more active and yang or passive and yin.	**POSITIONING** Place furniture and decorative objects where they will balance out the chi energies. Put more yang items in passive areas, more yin ones in active areas.

feng shui in practice

Positioning a large plant

You want to find the best location for a yucca. The plant is tall with long, tapering upward-pointing leaves. It is more yang and ideal for stimulating chi energy.

Solutions Because of the pointed leaves it will need plenty of space and should not be too close to seating or sleeping areas (to avoid cutting chi). A corner of a room where the chi energy might stagnate would be appropriate. The radiating shape represents fire chi energy. Green adds an element of tree energy, but the fiery appearance tends to override the colour in this case. Therefore, the yucca would be harmonious in a corner in the north-east, east, south-east, south or south-west of your home.

Choosing a living room sofa

You have decided to place a sofa in the west of your living room and you want one that will increase that area's romantic chi energy.

Solutions The shape of the west is round, the colour red and the material metal. A sofa that has rounded arms, a round back and metal feet or castors will increase the chi energy of the west. Red will also increase it. Complementary colours are white, yellow, black and grey. As red is a strong colour it need only be part of a pattern on the upholstery or on the cushions.

Finding an ideal bed

You need to buy a suitable bed to place in the south-east of your home so that the top of your head points east. The natural prevailing chi energy here is tree energy.

Solutions Materials, colours and shapes harmonious with the south-east are glass and wood, cream, green, blue and purple; irregular, tall and pointed. The ideal bed would therefore be raised off the ground (tall), with a natural wooden frame, and either painted in an appropriate colour or made up with cream, green, blue or purple bed linen.

Positioning a lamp

You have seen a free-standing lamp on a tall, thin, black metal frame, which you would like to buy, and you are wondering where to put it. Light itself is active and yang, and represents fire chi energy. The tall, thin shape produces tree chi energy, the material metal chi energy and the colour soil energy. The most active ingredient is yang fire chi energy.

Solutions The ideal location is a dark corner where the chi energy is more passive. In the north-east, east, south-east, south or south-west sector of your home or room, the light will harmonize with Five-Element fire energy. So a dark corner in any of those locations would be a suitable place for it – but especially in the north-east and south-west where soil and metal energies are in harmony.

using colour

Colours influence the light frequencies present in your home and will change your chi energy, whether they are used to paint walls, woodwork and furniture, or in soft furnishings such as curtains and upholstery, or in decorative objects. Even small amounts of a strong colour can have an effect. Colours can be related to yin and yang, the Five Elements and the Eight Directions (see pages 14, 18 and 22). Many Feng Shui practitioners use the Five Element colours, but I have found their relationship with the Eight Directions to be the most significant. Together with the centre, this gives you a palette of nine basic colours.

The outer ring of the colour wheel (page 74) shows the colours associated with the Eight Directions. These are the most strengthening colours for each direction. They maintain chi energy, which is a desirable aim if the chi energy there is favourable. Other colours can be used to enhance or calm chi energy in a particular direction. The chart opposite summarizes these relationships.

CHOOSING COLOURS

Colours can be used in two ways: as backgrounds over large areas and as accent colours in small areas. Background colours tend to be softer, paler shades, though this does not have to be the case, and accent colours tend to be stronger and more vivid, though again not necessarily. In Feng Shui terms, both uses can be effective if they are the right colours. The stronger the colour, the less you need for it to be effective. A small red cushion on a chair to the west of the centre of the room will be enough to enhance the chi energy associated with romance, contentment and income. To have the same effect, a soft pink would need to be used over a larger area such as a wall, large sofa or carpet.

The colours specified in the harmonious colours chart and shown in the colour wheel represent a range of colours rather than a single hue. Different shades and tones of these same colours share their harmonious qualities but carry a variety of nuances. For example, brighter shades are more yang than paler shades. Personal preference also has a part to play; if a colour has unpleasant associations for you, it would not be wise to use it whatever the charts advise. So, when choosing actual colours for a specific function, do not interpret the charts too rigidly.

harmonious colours

Ascertain the direction of the room you want to decorate, then choose a colour. Those in bold type are the most important. Yellow is harmonious in any direction.

DIRECTION	ENHANCE	STRENGTHEN	CALM
NORTH	red to pink white to grey	**off-white to cream**	pale green dark green to blue
NORTH-EAST	purple	brilliant white **yellow to brown** black	red to pink white to grey
EAST	off-white to cream	**bright green** dark green to blue	pale purple
SOUTH-EAST	off-white to cream	**dark green to blue** bright green	pale purple
SOUTH	bright green dark green to blue	**purple**	brilliant white pale yellow to brown, black
SOUTH-WEST	purple	black yellow to brown brilliant white	red to pink white to grey
WEST	brilliant white yellow to brown black	**red to pink** white to grey	off-white to cream
NORTH-WEST	brilliant white yellow to brown black	**white to grey** red to pink	off-white to cream

colour wheel

Each of the Eight Directions (pages 22–25) and its characteristic chi energy is associated with a particular colour, shown on the outer section of the wheel below. Using that colour in that direction in furnishings or decor will maintain the chi energy there. The inside ring shows the colours associated with the Five Elements which can be used as alternatives to the Eight Directions colours.

Different shades can produce subtle changes in the chi energy of an area. The swatches opposite show a variety of accent and background colours and their potential effects in certain rooms.

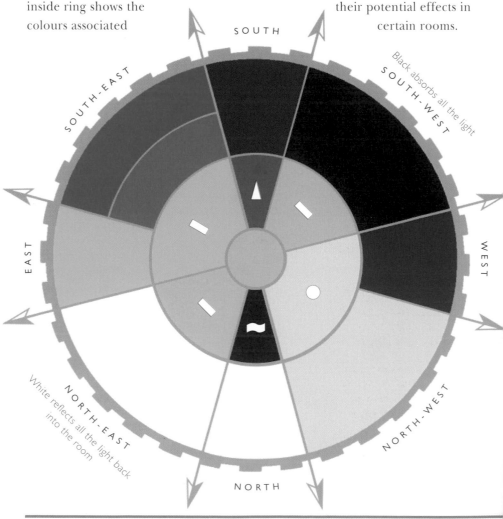

ACCENT COLOURS

Emerald green This best represents the tree energy of the south-east. Warmer yellowy tones give it a lively excitement that is also comforting.

Turquoise Closest to tree chi energy of the south-east, this is more yin and creates a relaxing atmosphere that is still vibrant and uplifting.

Deep blue Linked with the tree energy of the south-east, this strong blue would suit a sunny room. It helps to create a harmonious atmosphere.

Violet Very close to fire chi energy of the south, this hot fiery purple brings passion to a room. Good for sociability.

Peach pink The colour of sunset and closest to western metal energy, this enhances playfulness and romance – good for evening dining.

Orange This hot sunny colour is closest to the metal and soil chi energies of the west and centre. Creates a bright atmosphere in dark areas.

Chocolate Close to the metal and soil chi energies of the west and south-west, this enhances stability. Good in sunny rooms.

Mid grey Closest to the metal energy of the north-west, this enhances feelings of dignity and authority and creates a more formal atmosphere.

BACKGROUND COLOURS

Citron A sunny colour but with a lightly sharp edge, this is close to the soil energy of the centre. It evokes envigorating freshness and warmth.

Lime green Closest to eastern tree energy, this symbolizes new growth and produces a bright optimistic atmosphere. Good for young people.

Eau de nil Closest to south-eastern tree chi energy, this mix of watery blue and green is yin and peaceful. Good for creativity and relaxation.

Powder blue This soft pastel blue creates a more yin gentler flow of the normally uplifting tree energy. Soothing in bathrooms and kitchens.

Lavender Close to southern fire chi energy, but too pale to evoke passion, this has a more yin, mildly stimulating aura. Good for socializing.

Sugar pink Closest to the metal energy of the west, pink enhances a youthful, playful atmosphere.

Pale apricot This is closest to the soil energy of the centre, with a hint of western metal energy. Good for bedrooms.

Biscuit A quiet, light brown shade which enhances feelings of stability and security, this colour is closest to the soil energy of the centre.

using pattern

Patterned wallpaper, carpets, curtains and soft furnishings influence the nature and movement of chi energy in each room. The effect of different patterns is determined by the association of the shapes in them with yin and yang and the Five Elements. Similarly, the shapes in paintings, sculptures and other decorative objects will also have an influence (see page 80). If the pattern or shape is combined with its associated colour – for example, pointed patterns in purple, or circular patterns in red – the effects will be stronger.

PATTERNED WALLS

Walls are generally painted or papered. Plain painted walls are more yang than patterned walls. Irregular patterns produced by decorative paint effects such as sponging, colour-washing, rag-rolling and stippling are associated with Five-Element water energy, and create a more peaceful relaxing atmosphere. The use of creams, blues and greens would accentuate the calming effect.

Pattern is usually added to walls in the form of wallpaper, but stencilling, stamping and mural painting can do this too. Sharply defined, ordered and repeat patterns are more yang. Less defined, irregular or all-over mottled patterns are more yin. If patterns are pictorial (flowers, fruit, animals, country scenes) or have symbolic significance (stars, suns and moons), make sure the images have positive associations for you.

PATTERNED SOFT FURNISHINGS

The principles of choosing patterned fabric are the same as for choosing wallpaper. First check the direction of the curtains, soft furnishings or furniture from the centre of the room. Then, decide whether you want to maintain, enhance or calm the chi energy there. Consult the chart on page 73 for harmonious colours and the chart opposite to determine which patterns or shapes are harmonious.

Influential patterns
The basic pattern groups can be linked with Five-Element chi energies: (from top to bottom) irregular patterns with water, vertical stripes with tree, stars with fire, checks with soil and rounded patterns with metal.

harmonious patterns and shapes

DIRECTION	ENHANCE		STRENGTHEN		CALM	
NORTH		circles arches ovals		irregular clouds waves		tall and thin vertical stripes
NORTH-EAST		pointed stars zigzags		wide rectangles horizontal stripes checks		circles arches ovals
EAST		irregular clouds waves		tall and thin vertical stripes		pointed stars zigzags
SOUTH-EAST		irregular clouds waves		tall and thin vertical stripes		pointed stars zigzags
SOUTH		tall and thin vertical stripes		pointed stars zigzags		wide rectangles horizontal stripes. checks
SOUTH-WEST		pointed stars zigzags		wide rectangles horizontal stripes checks		circles arches ovals
WEST		wide rectangles horizontal stripes checks		circles arches ovals		irregular clouds waves
NORTH-WEST		wide rectangles horizontal stripes checks		circles arches ovals		irregular clouds waves

harmonious materials

To assess the effects of objects you wish to position, consider the materials they are made of. Plastic carries fire energy, but is undesirable in Feng Shui terms.

DIRECTION	ENHANCE	STRENGTHEN	CALM
NORTH	metal, harder stone	glass	wood wicker, bamboo, rattan plant fibres
NORTH-EAST	(plastic)	ceramic and clay, softer stone, fabric	metal harder stone
EAST	glass	wood bamboo, rattan plant fibres	(plastic)
SOUTH-EAST	glass	wood bamboo, rattan plant fibres	(plastic)
SOUTH	wood, wicker, bamboo, rattan plant fibres	(plastic)	ceramic and clay softer stone fabric
SOUTH-WEST	(plastic)	ceramic and clay, softer stone, fabric	metal harder stone
WEST	ceramic and clay, softer stone, fabric	metal harder stone	glass
NORTH-WEST	ceramic and clay, softer stone, fabric	metal harder stone	glass

lighting

Light waves bring energy into a space and help activate the ambient chi energy there. Artificial light is usually harsher than candlelight. Ideally, windows and skylights should be large enough to let in plenty of natural light during the day, so that artificial light is confined to evenings and dark days. Pale colours on the walls and carefully placed mirrors can reflect sunlight into a room.

TYPES OF LIGHTING

INCANDESCENT LIGHT-BULBS Used for general household lighting, these give a broad angle of uniform light. They increase the chi energy over a wide area in a relatively even manner.

SPOTLIGHTS These allow you to focus light in a particular place, enabling you to activate chi energy in specific areas like dark corners, which are at risk of stagnation. Use them also to illuminate one area of a multi-purpose room for work while the rest of the room remains in natural or more subdued lighting.

UP-LIGHTERS These encourage an upward flow of chi energy, which is particularly helpful if you have a low or sloping ceiling.

LOW VOLTAGE LIGHTING Ideal for increasing the flow of chi energy through stagnant areas, this produces a bright high-intensity light. It is easily recessed into ceilings and is also much used in free-standing lamps, which can be used for up- or down-lighting.

FLUORESCENT LIGHTING This emits a different colour of light and also gives off more electrical radiation. In my view this can lead to headaches, loss of concentration and mental tiredness. The same applies to small energy-saving fluorescent bulbs.

COLOURED LIGHTING This introduces a particular frequency of light. Check the direction of coloured lights from the centre of your home, and choose a harmonious colour from the chart on page 73.

Lampshades
Metal, glass or reflective shades create a less relaxing, more yang atmosphere; with fabric or paper shades it is softer and more yin.

decorative objects

The flow of chi energy in your home and garden is affected by any sculptures, works of art or decorative objects you place there. This includes paintings as well as three-dimensional items. The influence of an object depends largely on its shape and material. Images can also have an effect by their symbolic meaning, which influences your own flow of chi energy. A picture or sculpture of a couple in a loving embrace, for example, can encourage feelings of romance in you.

The influence of different shapes, colours and materials on chi energy is described on pages 72–8. By putting combinations of these properties together you can devise the ideal statue or sculpture for the effect you want.

Square boxes
These add metal energy. Use in the south-west to boost stability.

Clear glass
Place in the north to create a flowing atmosphere.

Shiny ceramics
Spherical shapes help concentrate energy in the west and north-west.

Clay birds
Low clay objects create a steady atmos-phere. Use in the north-east.

Wooden animals
These add liveliness which is harmonious in the east and south-east.

Metal boxes and frames
Use these to add solid metal energy in the north-west and west.

Stone figures
Romantic images boost the playful energy of the west.

flowers and plants

As decorative objects plants are special because they are living things that generate their own particular flow of chi energy. Healthy green plants create a fresher, more alive atmosphere and can compensate for the relatively dead materials often found in the home – electrical appliances that emit radiation and plastic and other synthetic materials that emit static energy. Plants also provide fresh air in the form of oxygen through their metabolic processes.

Different plants have different effects, depending largely on their overall shape, the shape of their leaves and flowers, and their colour, which associate them with the Eight Directions, the Five Elements of chi energy and yin and yang. Plants with pointed leaves are more yang and help to move chi energy more quickly. Plants with round floppy leaves are more yin and calm chi energy. Bushy plants help slow fast-moving chi energy and are effective in long corridors or near doors. Tall plants generate more tree chi energy, prickly plants and those with star-shaped pointed leaves encourage fire energy, low spreading plants produce soil energy, round plants or those with small round leaves metal energy, and trailing plants water energy. The green of the leaves also adds tree energy, but the colour of flowering plants adds more of the energy associated with that colour.

Fresh flowers also bring lively chi energy to your home. The colour and to a lesser extent the shape of the flowers will influence the nature of chi energy in that part of the room. Flowers are most effective if they are healthy and well looked after. Wilting flowers have a negative effect on chi energy so change the water daily and trim stems diagonally to make them last longer. Remove dead flowerheads and wilting foliage.

Although they are fashionable and popular in the West, dried flowers are less acceptable in Feng Shui terms since, for some people, they symbolize death and decay. Artificial flowers are recommended by Feng Shui practitioners if they are made of suitable material such as silk or paper. Neither dried or artificial flowers are as effective as living plants.

Radiation remedy
Indoor plants, like this peace lily (Spathyphyllum wallisii), can be placed next to electrical appliances to remedy their detrimental chi energy.

indoor plants

A variety of plants in the home give a more balanced flow of chi energy. Consider the plants' relationship to ying and yang and the Five Elements when placing them.

YANG

DRACAENA (*Dracaena marginata*) The strong upward growth with sharp pointed leaves combines tree and fire chi energies. This plant is good for stimulating chi in a corner or under a sloping ceiling, but do not place it close to where you sit or sleep. Ideal in the east, south-east, south and south-west.

WATER

IVY (*Hedera helix*) The bushiness, upward growth and floppy leaves make ivy relatively well-balanced. But its clinging trailing habit means that it generates water chi energy. It is useful in any area that lacks sunlight (such as an internal bathroom) because, unlike many plants, it grows in shade. The ideal position for it is in the north.

YIN

SPIDER PLANT (*Chlorophytum comosum*) The long, narrow, pointed leaves cascading downwards create a calming more yin atmosphere. Ideal in the north.
SWISS CHEESE PLANT (*Monstera deliciosa*) Large floppy leaves create a more yin soothing chi energy. This plant is ideal in any area that needs calming, especially the south, south-west and north-east.

TREE

HYACINTH (*Hyacinthus orientalis*) Straight upward-growing plants add uplifting tree chi energy. From the pink, white, blue or cream flowers, choose one in harmony with its position. this tree is especially harmonious in the east and south-east.

Money

Hyacinth

Poinsettia

FIRE

AFRICAN VIOLET (*Saintpaulia*) Purple star-shaped flowers make this plant strong in fire chi energy. It is helpful for attracting attention and getting public recognition for your efforts. The ideal positions are east, south-east, south, south-west and north-east.

PALM (*Phoenix roebelenii*) These upward-growing plants with spreading pointed leaves add fire chi energy and create a more yang active atmosphere. They are ideal for corners. Avoid placing in the north-east where the energy is already sharp and piercing. Ideal positions are east, south-east, south and south-west.

POINSETTIA (*Euphorbia pulcherrima*) The star-shaped leaf clusters can be red, pink, yellow or cream and the shape is linked with fire energy. Choose a colour to suit the location.

SOIL

CYCLAMEN (*Cyclamen persicum*) This spreading plant adds soil chi energy. Choose a purple flowering one for more passion in your life, a red or pink one for romance and excitement, and a white one for stability. The ideal positions for this plant are south, south-west, north-east, west and north-west.

EYELASH BEGONIA (*Begonia bowerae*) This white-flowering, low spreading plant creates more yin soil chi energy, which is good for a settled, stable atmosphere. The ideal positions are in the south, south-west, north-east, west and north-west of your home.

METAL

MONEY PLANT (*Crassula ovata*) Round thick leaves represent metal energy, which adds stability. The name is apt as metal chi energy helps finances. Ideal in the west, north-west and north.

PEACE LILY (*Spathiphyllum wallisii*) This counteracts electrical radiation from computers (see page 81).

Cyclamen

USING PLANTS

INTERNAL CORNERS Plants help avoid stagnation by getting chi energy moving. Use more yang plants associated with fire chi energy, especially those with long, sharp, pointed leaves.

PROTRUDING CORNERS Place bushy plants in front of corners to calm cutting chi (see page 8). Plants with round leaves and dense foliage are the most effective in this respect.

LONG CORRIDORS Stagger bushy plants either side of a long corridor to slow fast-moving chi.

BATHROOMS Plants here help keep chi energy moving. Tall plants increase tree energy and help drain excess water energy, especially if they are in the north of the room.

KITCHENS Plants add natural living energy to food preparation and storage areas. Tall plants add tree chi energy which is in harmony with the water and fire energies of the sink and cooker.

BEDROOMS Plants add healthy natural chi in bedrooms, some of which you absorb as you sleep. More yin, floppy plants help create a calm atmosphere.

SECURITY Prickly plants such as cacti give off a spiky energy which can deter burglars. Place them along window sills.

flowers

If you feel the chi energy in part of a room or your home generally needs boosting, use the following: cream flowers in the north, white flowers in the north-east, tall greenery in the east, tall blue flowers or greenery in the south-east, star-shaped purple flowers in the south, low yellow flowers in the south-west and centre, round red flowers in the west, and round white flowers in the north-west.

Tulip
The bowl-shaped blooms carry metal energy. Red in the west adds romance, pink in the west brings pleasure, white brings motivation in the north-east, dignity in the north-west, and peace in the north.

Iris
These come in many colours especially yellows, blues and purples. In spite of these links with tree energy and with the centre and south, their delicate appearance gives them a more yin quality. Use them to introduce vitality and passion, but gently.

Sunflower
The jagged flower shape has fire chi energy, but yellow is closer to soil energy. They spread out chi and have a powerful stabilizing influence.

Different flowers for different chi energies
Depending on their colour and shape, flowers enhance the chi energy of particular directions.

Carnation
The round shape of the flowers and the reds and pinks enhance romance and pleasure, whereas white adds dignity and serenity.

Mimosa
Flowers composed of many small yellow spheres increase the chi energy of the centre. Place them in the centre of your home to keep your life more centred.

Anemone
The shape is linked with metal energy and this, with strong colours, helps keep chi energy in one place. Red anemones in a west-facing bathroom could help prevent chi from draining away.

Lily
Despite the tall stems, the flowers often point downwards giving them a more settling influence. Use them to quieten an over-active part of your home.

Daisy
The round white flowers are harmonious in northern locations. In the north they add tranquillity, in the north-west dignity, and in the north-east motivation.

Rose
Tight round rosebuds are linked with metal energy, but as they open this changes to a more fiery shape. Red roses will increase the chi energy of romance and style, especially if placed in the west.

furniture

People often buy furniture that seems ideal in the store, but somehow does not feel right once they get it home. Feng Shui can help you choose furniture that is harmonious with its intended position. It helps you understand why certain items seem out of place, how to find the right furniture to fill difficult spaces, and how to find the best position for an existing piece of furniture. Check the relevant charts for harmonious colours, shapes and materials (pages 73, 77, 78).

Obviously, in some cases, practical considerations may override the requirements of Feng Shui and you need to compromise. Where materials are concerned, you can choose wood for any part of the home since its effect is largely neutral. If you were looking for a bedroom chair for the north-west of your home, for example, you would probably reject the harmonious materials (metal, stone) on practical grounds and choose wood, but a round, upholstered shape covered in a circular-patterned fabric in grey and pink shades would also be an ideal choice.

New furniture contributes a fresh, virgin atmosphere to a home whereas old furniture has absorbed chi energy from the past and has a more substantial feel. The kind of chi energy absorbed depends on the past use of the piece. A butcher's table will have absorbed a different kind of chi energy to a table used for displaying china. Find out the history of old pieces and make sure that it is compatible with your intentions for it. Most furniture will take in the chi energy of its new environment within a short time. Exercise particular caution with furniture that has been used for the slaughter of animals, or comes from funeral parlours, hospitals or similar environments.

Avoid positioning furniture so that sharp edges point towards you. This can direct swirling chi energy, known as cutting chi, towards you which causes your own chi energy to swirl and can lead to feelings of disorientation and eventually ill-health. Also avoid over-furnishing or filling rooms with clutter, which make it harder for chi energy to circulate and may lead to stagnation

TYPES OF FURNITURE

BEDS Bedrooms with high ceilings can take high beds on legs, which enhances uplifting tree chi energy. Bedrooms with lower ceilings would be better served by a low beds or futons. These create a more settled, soil chi energy. (See also page 49.)

CHAIRS Rounded, soft, plump chairs are more yin and therefore more relaxing. Upright, straight-backed chairs are more yang and activating. Mix more yin and more yang chairs to create a balanced atmosphere. Use colours to create a contrast, for example a red yang cushion on a soft yin chair.

TABLES The shape of a dining table has a strong influence on the area used for eating (see page 42). Side tables and coffee tables should have rounded corners, especially if they are placed in seating areas, to avoid cutting chi. Yang materials, such as glass on the table top, will speed up the flow of chi energy and produce a more stimulating, wideawake atmosphere; yin materials such as light natural wood will have a more soothing effect.

DRAWERS Tall chests of drawers encourage a greater flow of upward tree chi energy whereas low wide chests of drawers bring out more settled soil chi energy. Round knobs, particularly if made of metal, enhance metal chi energy and give a chest a more solid feel.

DRESSING TABLES If this is in the bedroom it should have rounded corners to avoid cutting chi. Do not let the mirror face your bed during the night. Cover it with a cloth when you go to bed if necessary. An oval mirror matches the outline of your head and is better for feeling more relaxed while putting on make-up.

CUPBOARDS Built-in cupboards should be designed to avoid stagnation. Hard, smooth, shiny surfaces help to keep chi energy moving. Where possible they should square off a room. For instance, you might build the cupboards into an alcove to eliminate the corners of the alcove and avoid introducing more sharp corners into the room. This is particularly important in bedrooms. Place free-standing cupboards in alcoves, too, if possible, for the same reasons. Corner cupboards are particularly helpful as they cut off internal corners without adding any protruding corners.

Yang chairs
Ideal for a home office where you need to be alert and stimulated, yang chairs have hard shiny surfaces and are made of metal or dark polished hardwoods.

Yin chairs
Padded furniture with smooth, curved outlines and soft fabric coverings is more yin, ideal for living rooms and bedrooms where you need to relax and wind down.

windows

Windows allow chi energy to flow easily into and out of your home, and they let in light. The direction the light comes from changes the chi energy in your home so eastern sunlight, for example, is very different from western sunlight. To determine the chi energy entering through the windows, place the grid of the Eight Directions over your floor plan and check their locations.

Ideally, the windows should expose your home to light from all directions. Where this is not possible, you might like to consider installing skylights. These are a useful means of bringing in more light, especially in rooms with no windows.

Make sure all your windows are easy to open. Ideally, open them at least once a day throughout the year to allow fresh air and chi energy into your home, and make sure you clean them regularly. Replace cracked or broken panes promptly.

Finally, avoid sitting with your back to a window or sleeping near a window unless it is covered with thick curtains. Both these situations can be unsettling and make it difficult for you to relax or go to sleep.

window treatments

The type of window covering you have eases or inhibits the entry of chi energy into a room.

Curtains
When drawn in large rooms, full curtains create a cosy atmosphere, but in small rooms they entail a risk of stagnation. Curtains in bedrooms help you sleep.

Vertical blinds
These are associated with tree chi energy and are useful if you want to make the room seem taller.

TYPES OF WINDOW

Chi energy enters and leaves a home more easily through large windows, but too many windows encourages too great a movement, making the home difficult to relax in. Too few or small windows can cause chi energy to slow down and stagnate. Ideally, the number of windows should be balanced against their size, and the type of glass used can help to counteract any disadvantages of size. The window's shape is related to Five-Element chi energy and also has an effect.

Tall rectangular windows represent tree energy, producing an upward-moving atmosphere in the home. They are most harmonious in the east, south and south-east of the home.

Pointed or triangular windows represent fire energy but are rarely found in domestic buildings.

Wide rectangular or square windows create a more settled atmosphere. They are linked to soil energy and are best sited to the south, south-west, west, north-west or north-east.

Round windows are linked to metal energy. They create a more concentrated atmosphere and are most applicable to the south-west, west, north-west, north and north-east.

Venetian blinds
These prevent stagnation. They allow in plenty of light so are good for small windows. Wooden blinds have a neutral effect on chi; metal speeds it up and plastic blocks the flow.

Roller blinds
Similar in their effects to slatted blinds, these create a slightly softer atmosphere because of the fabric. Use coloured or patterned fabric appropriate to the direction.

Shutters
More light is shut out by these coverings than any others and, as they are relatively solid, their influence on the flow of chi energy is similar to that of walls.

mirrors

Mirrors are very important in Feng Shui. They speed up and redirect the flow of chi energy. The hard, flat, shiny surfaces help chi energy to move more quickly, and their reflective quality deflects some of the chi in other directions. The effect is similar to the way they redirect light waves. Mirrors can therefore be used to direct chi energy and light to a part of your home where chi energy is stagnant. They can also reflect energy away from an area that has an excess of chi energy and deflect channels of fast-moving chi energy, unfavourable chi or cutting chi.

Mirrors are the most effective objects in these respects, but anything with a reflective surface can influence the flow of chi energy in a similar way. Flat items, such as the glass in a framed picture, act like flat mirrors; shaped items, such as door knockers, like convex mirrors (see below). The more polished and reflective the surface, the stronger the effect on chi energy. They can be used like mirrors (see opposite), and are also useful in dark areas such as corners to keep chi energy moving.

To deflect cutting chi from sharp corners or busy road away from your home, use shiny reflective door fittings. These are more practical alternatives to mirrors.

MIRROR SHAPES

Flat and convex are the two types of mirrors used in Feng Shui. Flat mirrors redirect chi energy in one direction whereas convex mirrors spread it out in lots of directions. Convex mirrors are usually round, but flat ones can be rectangular, square, round, oval, octagonal and irregular. Octagonal mirrors have special significance in Feng Shui as the eight sides are in harmony with the Eight Directions, but the other shapes can also be significant, and the material and colour of the mirror frame can also have a subtle influence on the surrounding chi.

Circular and oval mirrors are associated with metal chi energy, but whereas circles are more yang and help to contain chi, oval mirrors are more yin and therefore tend to disperse chi. Tall, thin rectangular shapes encourage upward-moving tree chi energy. Low, wide rectangles are associated with soil energy and create a more stable, settled atmosphere in a room. Like circles, squares are compact shapes and have the effect of containing chi energy.

using mirrors

Mirrors are used in many Feng Shui remedies. Positioned carefully, they can help chi energy to move harmoniously through your home, and overcome the disadvantages of problem features such as long narrow corridors, small or L-shaped rooms and stairs opposite the front door.

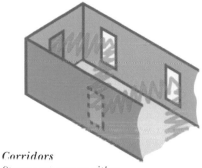

Corridors

Stagger mirrors on either side of a long corridor to move chi energy from side to side, slowing the flow. The corridor will also appear wider. In a dark, winding corridor position a convex mirror on the bend so that you can see around it. If daylight is reflected in it so much the better; the mirror also helps chi flow round the bend.

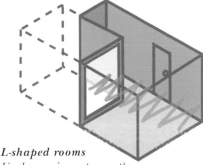

L-shaped rooms

Use large mirrors to give the impression a room extends into an indentation. Hang them to reflect the space facing the mirror into the indentation. They will also encourage chi to flow across the room, making the mirror wall seem further away.

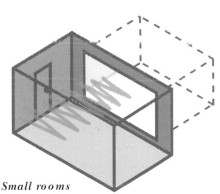

Small rooms

Large flat mirrors can make a narrow room appear wider by directing the chi energy across the room.

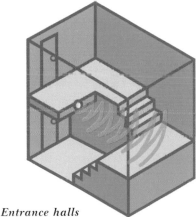

Entrance halls

Where stairs are positioned opposite the front door, place a convex mirror to reflect chi energy back into the house. Place a large flat mirror next to the front door so you see round the door as you open it.

other chi activators

Certain small items can be used to activate chi in a variety of contexts and in a particularly powerful way. These include crystals, lighted candles, things that make beautiful sounds and sea salt.

CRYSTALS

As sunlight passes through a crystal it refracts into the colours of the rainbow. Beams of coloured light radiate in all directions, each colour carrying the intensity of that particular type of chi energy.

The commonest crystals are round multi-faceted ones. Irregularly shaped or jagged crystals can also be used but take care to avoid creating too much spiky chi. Place them near plants whose own yin chi energy will help smooth that of the crystal.

CANDLES

Candles have fire chi energy, which encourages passion and helps attract attention. If you want to develop a more intimate relationship with someone, place a pair of candles close together. Tall ones are the most suitable as they represent tree energy which is supportive to fire.

The most favourable locations for candles are in the east, south-east, south, south-west, centre and north-east of your home or particular room. You can keep the candle burning continuously, or while you are in the room, or when that direction is most active (see pages 22–25).

Candles are helpful where a home or room is lacking sunlight. Place several candles in the south of the room or in the corner. In dark damp rooms candles make the atmosphere drier and brighter.

The shape, material and colour of the candle holder has a subtle influence on the surrounding chi energy. A tall, black, wrought iron holder, for example, is associated with tree, soil and metal chi energies. A tall, green, wooden holder has tree chi energy characteristics, and a flat white china holder soil chi energy.

White candles have the closest relationship to the flame of the candle and, in most situations, are preferable to coloured candles.

Using crystals
Hung in a window, crystals can bring chi energy from outside into dark or stagnant areas of your home.

SOUNDS

Sound vibrates the air, which stimulates chi energy. Chanting and singing can achieve this, but wind chimes, bells and gongs, ticking clocks and the sound of running water are also helpful.

WIND CHIMES   The tone is intended to purify and cleanse chi energy, so choose chimes carefully for the sweetness and clarity of their sound. Chimes are usually made of metal, wood or pottery, which enhance the elements of metal, tree and soil respectively.

When you have decided where the chimes should be, check that direction from the centre of your home and choose an appropriate material (see page 78). To stimulate chi energy near a door in the north of your home, for example, hang metal chimes so that they sound when the door is opened. To calm chi energy of the south, pottery chimes are more suitable.

BELLS AND GONGS   Traditionally, these have been used to clear chi energy in a part or all of the home. They can be rung by hand in areas that feel heavy or stagnant. Other ringing sounds have a similar effect. If the sound is generated by a metal bell rather than electronically, telephone and door bells can enhance the flow of chi energy.

Making sounds
Whether loud or soft, sounds can stimulate or cleanse chi energy, particularly in areas where it is prone to stagnation (dark corners, corridors, hallways or under sloping roofs).

SEA SALT

Salt is the most yang of the foods we eat. It is found in blood in the form of sodium and thus has a direct influence on your personal chi energy. It also has the ability to draw moisture out of the atmosphere, and in Feng Shui terms its effect is to pull chi energy into it, which tends to have a purifying and stabilizing influence. This contracting inward-moving chi is associated with Five-Element metal energy, so you can use sea salt in situations where it will be in harmony with that. Place one or two tablespoons of salt in a low white china bowl. Place the bowl on the floor, or on a shelf or table if you have children or pets. Alternatively, tuck it out of sight behind a piece of furniture

Sea salt is most effective in the north-east and south-west of the house where the metal energy of the salt will help stabilize the naturally less stable flow of soil chi.

water features

Water is one of the key solutions in Feng Shui as it has a special significance for the human body: it carries ingredients vital for human life
and is essential for growing food. Humans evolved from sea creatures
and most of our body weight is made up of water. By adding a water
feature either to your garden or inside your home you bring in fresh chi
energy that can be highly beneficial for your health and destiny.

The water feature can take the form of a garden pond, fountain,
swimming pool, bird bath, aquarium, or other indoor water feature.
Even a small bowl of fresh clean water can be effective. The water
should remain fresh and unpolluted. Place it either east or south-east
from the centre of your home; no other locations are recommended.

An aquarium is a favourite means of bringing moving water indoors.
Place the tank east or south-east from the centre of your home and, if
possible, to the east or south-east from the centre of the room. Use
pebbles and shells rather than plastic decoration. Appropriate living
plants in the water will add their own chi energy and help keep the tank
clean and the fish healthy.

Indoor fountains can vary from elaborate structures to a small rock
with an integral pump that moves water to the top of the rock and allows
it to trickle down again. As with aquariums, these should be located to
the east or south-east of the centre of your home or room.

If you do not have the space for a more elaborate water feature place
a bowl of water to the east or south-east of your
home. Refill it each day. Ideally, the bowl should
be refilled from a tap in the east or south-east
of the home before any other water is
taken from it.

FISH
Depending on their shape, colour and behaviour, the fish
you put into a aquarium can either be more yin or more yang.
Quick, aggressive fish darting backwards and forwards will create a
more yang dynamic flow of chi. Brightly coloured fish are also stimulating. Slow, peaceful fish, or fish with muted colours are more yin
and promote a gentler more relaxing atmosphere.

Acknowledgements

Carroll and Brown would like to thank the following:

Illustrations: D. Brown, Peter Cambell, Karen Cochrane
Model Making: Robert Bradshaw
Photography: David Murray, Jules Selmes
Design: Vimit Punater
Editorial: Madeleine Jennings
Production: Wendy Lawson

Author acknowledgements:

I would like to thank all those who have played their part in helping me to arrive at the place where I could write this book: all the Browns, especially my mother Patsy, Dragana, the love of my life, my children Christopher, Alexander, Nicholas and Michael, also Adam and Angela and their children; the Waxmans, especially Melanie and Denny for getting me started; an enormous thank you to Boy George for all his help; my friends and clients Kim Andreoli, Adrienne Brown, Jasna Cacik, Enno and Dusica von Landmann, Michael Maloney, the Mosbachers, and my oldest friend Jeremy Parkin; my teachers and colleagues Michio and Aveline Kushi, Shizuko Yamamoto; my colleagues Maria and John Brosnan; Stephen Skinner and Nimita Palmer at *Feng Shui for Modern Living*; Jon Sandifer and everyone at the Feng Shui Society; a special thank you to all my clients who have given me the opportunity to put Feng Shui into practice; and everyone at Carroll and Brown, especially Amy Carroll, Denise Brown and Madeleine Jennings.

Simon Brown

about the author

Simon Brown began his career as a design engineer and has had two inventions patented in his name. In 1981 he began studies in Oriental medicine and qualified as a shiatsu therapist and macrobiotic consultant. In addition to these healing arts, he studied Feng Shui. For seven years he was director of London's Community Health Foundation, a charity that ran a wide range of courses specialising in Japanese and Chinese healing arts. During this time Simon taught the first courses on Feng Shui to the UK general public. Simon has since made Feng Shui his full-time career. His client list ranges from large public companies (such as British Airways and The Body Shop) to celebrities (including Boy George). Presently, he writes regular features for the magazine *Feng Shui for Modern Living* and conducts training workshops in Lisbon, Munich, Paris, Rome and various cities throughout the UK and US.

All books by Simon Brown use the compass style of Feng Shui.

Also published by Ward Lock:

Practical Feng Shui
A complete do-it-yourself practical guide to Feng Shui. Explains how Feng Shui works with full colour photographs and drawings. Expanding on the material covered in *Essential Feng Shui*, this book provides additional information on how to carry out a Feng Shui survey and further design solutions for your home. It advises on how to make the most of the shape and location of your home, how best to tackle unusual areas such as utility and storage rooms, staircases, doors and fireplaces, and helps you to understand the effects of sunlight. It also includes information on Feng Shui astrology, based on the Nine Ki system.

Practical Feng Shui for Business
Ideal for anyone who wants to apply Feng Shui to their career. This book explains how to be more successful at work. Full of colourful drawings and photographs to help you to implement Feng Shui in real life situations, the book also includes successful strategies for offices, shops and restaurants.

Practical Feng Shui Astrology
Using the Nine Ki system, learn how to make and read your own birth chart, which can then be used to gain interesting insights into your relationships with lovers, friends and family. This book helps you to work out the best time to make important changes in your life and highlights the most favourable times of year for you. Also in full colour with quick reference charts that make it fun and easy to use.

Other publications include:

The Principles of Feng Shui
(Thorsons ISBN 0 7225 3347 0)
This is now also available as an audio cassette.

For information on Feng Shui consultations and courses with Simon Brown contact:
PO Box 10453, London NW3 4WD, England.
Tel/Fax 00-44-207-431 9897
e-mail 106025.3515@compuserve.com.

Visit his web site, including software for floor plans and Nine Ki information, on:
HTTP://ourworld.compuserve.com/homepages/simonbrown_fengshui